Nomads of Niger

Photographs by
CAROL BECKWITH

Text by
MARION VAN OFFELEN

HARRY N. ABRAMS, INC., PUBLISHERS, NEW YORK

On preceding pages:

A Wodaabe male arrayed for the *geerewol* dance—
a contest whose winner is judged most handsome

A herdsman regrouping his animals at Eggo Well

A young unmarried woman *(surbaajo)* festively
attired for rainy season celebrations

A *surbaajo* dressed for her role as observer–judge
at the *geerewol* dance

Youths *(sukaabe)* vying in charm in the *yaake* dance

Close-ups of two *yaake* dancers displaying the whiteness of their eyes and teeth, criteria of beauty

Wodaabe and Tuareg nomads at a rainy season
gathering

The winner of a camel race

On these pages:

In search of pasturage and water, Wodaabe move
their cattle, sheep, and goats

A portion of the royalties from the sale of this book
will be used to assist the Wodaabe in times of extreme
drought.

Project Director: Robert Morton
Editor: Ruth Eisenstein
Designer: Patrick Cunningham
Drawings: Carol Beckwith
Translated from the French by Margaret Megaw

LIBRARY OF CONGRESS CATALOGING IN PUBLICATION DATA

Beckwith, Carol.
  Nomads of Niger.

  1. Fulahs—Pictorial works.   2. Nomads—Niger—
Pictorial works.   I. Offelen, Marion van.
II. Title.
DT547.45.F84B43 1983   306′.089963   83-2729
ISBN 0–8109–0734–8

CONTENTS

The People Called Wodaabe   17

A Day in the Life   19

At Eggo Well   65

To Intawella Market   89

On the Move   113

The *Worso*   145

The *Geerewol*   173

ACKNOWLEDGMENTS   224

THE PEOPLE CALLED
WODAABE

In central Niger, between the great Sahara Desert and the grasslands, lies an immense steppe, scattered with scrawny bushes and skeletal trees. For nine months of the year hardly a drop of rain falls. Ponds dry up and the water level in the wells gets lower and lower. Pastures disappear, seared by an implacable sun. The days are torrid, the nights sometimes freezing cold. And the harmattan, the hot wind out of the desert, blows up relentlessly, filling the air with a sandy haze.

Sporadically during the other three months of the year, the rains return, often preceded by terrifying storms. Grass sprouts again, the ponds slowly fill, leaves cover the trees, life is reborn. But soon the rains diminish, then end. And the all-powerful drought reassumes its ascendancy over this desertlike universe.

For all that, people live here, coming and going across this vast territory at the mercy of the climate and the limited means for survival it offers. They are the Wodaabe, commonly called Bororo, who number among the last nomads of Africa, indeed among the last nomads on earth. They are slender and long-limbed, with bronze skin and fine, delicate features. As a people they belong to the larger group of the Fulani, but of this group they constitute no more than a tiny minority. The Fulani (also called Peuls and Fulbe) are scattered through the area between Senegal and the Central African Republic. Among the Fulani the Wodaabe are virtually the only group that has preserved the ancient nomadic tradition; their one remaining bond with the other Fulani is their common language, Fulfulde. The power of tradition among the Wodaabe is indicated by their name, the literal meaning of which is "the people of the taboo."

Niger is a region of astonishing diversity of climates, landscapes, and ethnic groups. To the north stretches the desert: sand, sand, and more sand. From time to time, enormous black rock uplifts come into view like tortuously shaped islands jutting out of a petrified sea. Caravans of Tuareg camel drivers—the celebrated "blue men"—file across the dunes, bearing millet and salt.

To the south, the terrain is largely grasslands, with scattered trees. Because the rains here are more frequent, the savanna is fertile and is inhabited by farmers, notably the Hausa and the Djerma-Songhaï.

On the arid and inhospitable steppe that is the Wodaabe's domain, these nomadic herdsmen are continually on the move. They depend chiefly upon their herds of cattle for their subsistence but also own sheep, goats, donkeys, and camels. They are under constant pressure to find pasture and water for their animals, especially the zebu cattle, with whom they live in a totally symbiotic relationship. But they know the environment admirably well and have adapted their way of life to it perfectly.

The Wodaabe say of themselves that they live "like the birds in the bush." They never settle down. They leave no trace of their passage from encampment to encampment. The Wodaabe's habitations—small roofless semicircular shelters made of branches of thorny trees —melt into the natural surroundings like the nests of birds.

Choosing to live as nomads, the Wodaabe reject all efforts made to change their precarious way of life. They say that life is made up of suffering and joy: the hardship of the dry season alternates with the happiness of the rainy season. What is important is to have *munyal* (patience, fortitude) during the difficult periods. "Who cannot bear the smoke will never get to the fire," says a Wodaabe proverb.

The Wodaabe believe that the life they lead is the only one for them because it is the way of tradition. "Tradition is what binds us, keeps us alive, enables us to live together. From the moment we open our eyes, we follow the way of tradition, *mbodangaaku*. For tradition is a path, a path that must be followed. One who does not follow this path, who strays from it, is no longer a

---

OPPOSITE: A Wodaabe man wrapped against wind and sand in a five-meter-long turban.

Bodaado, one of the Wodaabe. Tradition is friendship, it is mutual assistance, it is respect for others. Tradition is a heritage we receive at birth and treasure until death. He who follows tradition is a Bodaado and he is free —for he is himself."

This respect for tradition is not of religious origin. Indeed, the Wodaabe's is not a deeply rooted religious disposition. They believe vaguely in a God, whom, under the influence of their Islamic neighbors, they call Allah. But while they pronounce the name of Allah under certain circumstances, in fact Allah represents only an ill-defined entity, the superior force that brings joy or hardship, suffering or happiness. Thus they invoke Allah in hard times or out of hope: "May Allah keep misfortune from us. . . . " "May Allah give you children. . . . " Anything the Wodaabe do not understand, like sickness or death, they attribute to supernatural forces identified only by the name of *ginni* (evil spirits of the bush). Tradition alone constitutes the faith that draws them together and enables them to live. They say "Tradition is happiness. It is what the heart wants, and to want happiness is life."

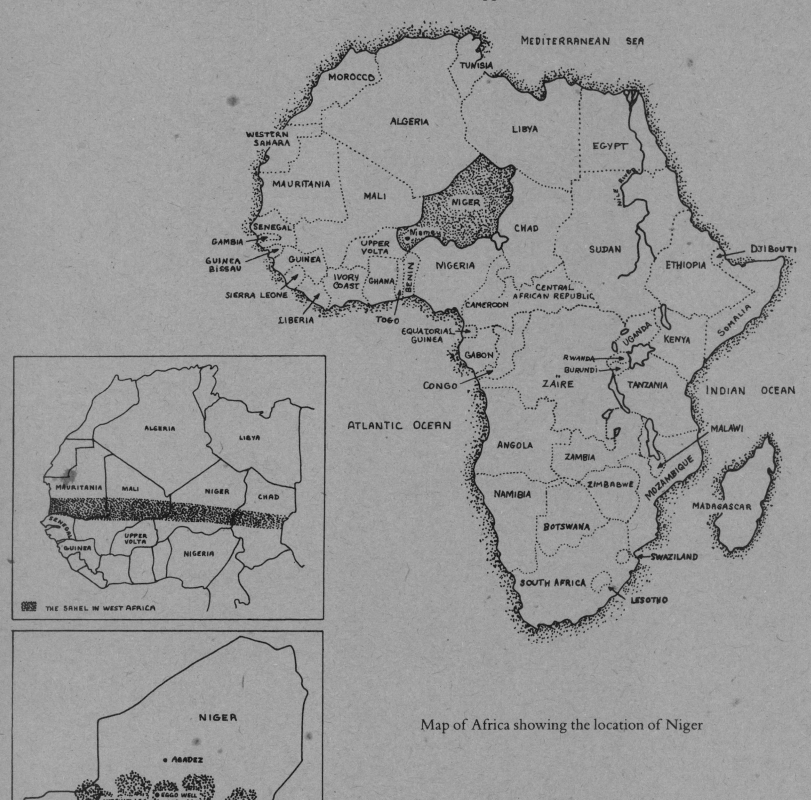

Map of Africa showing the location of Niger

A DAY IN THE LIFE

The oblique rays of the sun light up the sand stretching as far as the eye can see around the encampment. Here and there tufts of dry grasses and a few scraggly bushes dot the barren immensity of the Sahelian steppe as it appears in the dry season.

In the clear, still morning light, Mokao, as he does every day, leaves the bed where he and his wife, Mowa, sleep and rinses his face and hands. He goes next to take a look at his herd of zebus; they are grouped in a clearing beyond the rope to which the suckling calves are tethered. Then Mokao returns to sit on a mat near the bed and lights a small wood fire.

Mokao is slender and of medium height. He is about thirty years old. He is light-skinned, and his face is long, with a narrow nose and thin lips. His shoulder-length hair is arranged in numerous braids: two fairly thick ones on each side of his head, and fifteen other, thinner ones on the nape of his neck. Around his hips he wears a *dedo*, a tanned sheepskin, decorated with small silvery studs, one edge of which is drawn up between his legs; over this he wears a black tunic. To each side of Mokao's eyes, and alongside his nose and mouth, the bronzed skin of his face is tattooed with geometric designs denoting his Wodaabe identity. Mokao is a Bodaado of the Kasawsawa lineage ("the lineage of the long lance").

Mokao and his wife live in this encampment with his father, Gao, and his four brothers and their wives and children. The group migrates together throughout the year. In accordance with tradition, the encampment is lined up from south to north, each married woman having her own shelter (*suudu*), and the eldest occupying the southernmost position.

Still seated on his mat, Mokao, with a precise gesture, opens the bronze clasp of a large leather sack and takes out everything necessary for the preparation of tea: a metal tray, on which he places a small blue teapot, three tiny glasses, a cloth bag containing a cone-shaped sugar loaf, a metal rod to break up the sugar, and a box of China tea, his favorite kind. He piles up some embers from the fire in a brazier—a basket of woven iron wires mounted on a stand. He then fills his teapot with water, places it on the brazier, and pours in a glassful of tea leaves. He shakes the brazier to remove the ashes and fans the glowing embers with one of his sandals.

Meanwhile Mowa has risen from bed. She unties one of the calves from the calf rope and pushes it toward its mother. The calf quickly finds the udder and begins suckling greedily. After a few moments, Mowa pulls the calf away, ties it to the cow's left foreleg, squats down next to the cow with an ocher-colored calabash between her knees, and begins milking. The calabash is soon filled with fresh milk.

Mowa is about forty years old, tall and slender. She has high cheekbones, a thin, aquiline nose, and large black eyes. Her hair is elaborately plaited: two braids frame her face, and there is a knot on the top of her head and another braid at the nape of her neck. Nine large gleaming brass rings hang from each ear and jingle with her every movement. Around her neck she wears two necklaces of colored glass beads, the longer of which swings just above her bare breasts. She does not cover her breasts; married and the mother of several children, she may no longer appear flirtatious. It is only the young girls who are permitted the coquetry of wearing a blouse. Mowa wears wrapped around her a long piece of material made of strips of hand-woven cotton sewed together, secured at the waist by a narrow cloth cord. This wrapper, indigo blue shot through with light-blue threads, covers her legs to just below the knees. On her feet she wears flat leather sandals with thin leather thongs.

While Mowa milks the cows, Nebi, Mowa's daughter by a previous marriage, is seated on a mat in her mother's *suudu*, busy with her little eight-month-old daughter, Hadija. Nebi is married to Bango, the youngest of Mokao's four brothers. She is living here because, in accordance with tradition, when she was five months

Mokao's tea equipment

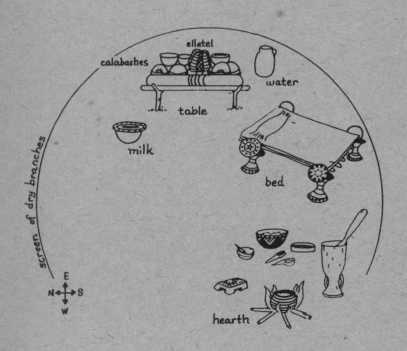

Plan of a *suudu*

pregnant she was required to leave her husband and to stay in her mother's *suudu*. The long leather necklace that Nebi wears, a talisman designed to "protect" her against men and guarantee the "good growth of her child," was given her by Mowa. As long as she wears it, Nebi may not have sexual relations with her husband or anyone else. She must remain in the encampment and help her mother with the daily chores. During this period she is called *boofiido* ("she who broods"). When Hadija is weaned, at the end of her second year, and Mowa decides that Nebi may resume normal relations with her husband, Mowa will remove the necklace. In accordance with age-old custom, she will take Nebi by surprise and tear the necklace off; Nebi will then hide for the day. Following this ritual, a family ceremony will be held to mark Nebi's formal accession to wifehood, and Nebi will at last establish her own *suudu*. Mowa will give her fifty calabashes, a bed, wrappers, and mats. In recognition of her new status, her husband, Bango, will braid a calf rope for her and will entrust his milk cows to her care.

When her calabash is full, Mowa unties the calf, permitting it to return to suckle its mother, and carries the receptacle toward the *suudu*, where she pours the frothy milk into another, larger calabash.

The *suudu* is Mowa's shelter and her domain. It contains everything she owns: her bed (four posts supporting two crossbeams overlaid by lengthwise poles covered with thick mats); a long, narrow wooden table (supported by four forked posts with poles resting in the forks). On the table are some fifty nested calabashes—five sets of ten, each set in a round basket woven of fibers of the doum palm *(Hyphenae thebaica)*. Atop the pile of calabashes is a large decorative structure made up of Mowa's *kaakol* and *elletel*. The *kaakol* consists of calabashes encased in tightly woven baskets adorned with silver studs and leather thongs, the whole supported on two wooden poles, which makes it portable. The *elletel* is a smaller version (about half as high) of the *kaakol*, which is about a meter in height. The *elletel* and the calabashes were given to Mowa by her mother, along with some ten mats, after the birth of her first child; the *kaakol* was a gift from her first husband's mother. These possessions are never used but constitute a woman's source of personal pride and prestige. Mowa displays them only on the occasion of the rainy season ceremonies, notably during the *worso*, the annual ceremony which brings together a part of Mokao's lineage and during which the year's births and marriages are celebrated.

Leather sacks behind the *kaakol* contain Mowa's wrappers and a small basket in which she keeps all her most precious personal possessions: jewelry, talismans, and various perfumes, and also powders made from plants, which are traditional medications. Beside the *kaakol* are the several calabashes for daily use bought by

Mowa at the market from the Hausa, who grow and prepare them.

Calabashes are made from the hard-rinded fruit of the calabash vine. When ripe, the gourds are harvested, dried, and cut open, most often in half, and the inside is carefully scraped out. Calabashes have many uses, depending on size and shape, and each type has its own individual name, denoting the use to which it is put. All these calabashes are the object of attentive care on the part of Wodaabe women. Using an awl, they decorate the outsides with geometric and other motifs: triangles, half moons, suns, sinuous lines. These designs, which are sometimes very elaborate, are passed down from generation to generation, but the details vary according to individual imagination and creativity. The designs engraved on the calabash are supposed to protect both the receptacle and its contents.

Mokao's two younger brothers, Bango and Amee, arrive from another part of the encampment. They wear large, wide-brimmed, conical hats trimmed with a brown leather band. Slung over his shoulder, each carries a Tuareg sword, its blade made of handworked steel and its sheath of waffled red leather, decorated with bits of copper and brass. They stop about a meter away from Mokao and exchange greetings, averting their eyes with an air of indifference, for to look the person one is addressing squarely in the face would indicate a lack of the reserve prescribed by Wodaabe tradition.

Mokao invites his brothers to sit down with him on the mat. Bango and Amee put down their swords and hats and remove their sandals before taking their places on the mat, where they sit cross-legged. Mokao hands each of them a glass of tea. There will be three rounds of tea in all. The first and strongest glass is "hard like life." The second, somewhat weaker, is "sweet like love." The third is "for pleasure." One may decline the first glass if one does not like strong tea, but if one accepts the second, one must drink the third.

Bango is the handsomest of the three men sitting on the mat and drinking tea. His long braids frame fine, regular features. When he smiles, dazzling white teeth light up his face. His appearance conforms to the very precise criteria by which the Wodaabe judge physical beauty. Light skin, a tall, slender body that is both spare and limber, and long, delicate hands go to make up their image of ideal beauty. The face must also be long and the forehead high; to raise the hairline, they shave the hair above the forehead. For the rest, the Wodaabe admire large eyes (considered all the more beautiful when the whites are sparklingly clear), a long, thin

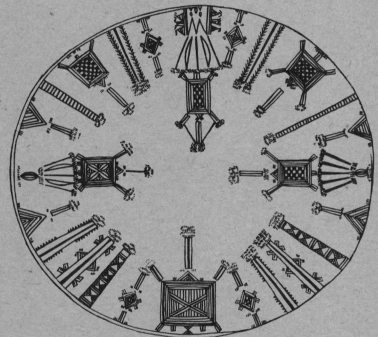

Traditional calabash designs. (After Chappel)

21

nose, thin lips, even teeth, which must also be very white, a long, supple neck, and straight hair.

Among the Wodaabe, beauty is of paramount importance, especially for the young men. Because it is the man's role to attract women, men spend more time than women adorning themselves and applying makeup. If a Bodaado is not handsome, he can compensate for this shortcoming with *togu*. The word denotes a combination of charm and seductiveness that has to do with one's way of being with others, one's manner of speaking, the sound of one's voice, one's sociability, enthusiasm, and sense of humor. A man or woman who has *togu* will attract the goodwill and friendship of others, and will never be alone. The Wodaabe say that *togu* comes from the heart: "He who has *togu* speaks with his heart."

The three brothers discuss the day's occupations. Bango and Amee will take the herds to the well, as they do every second day during the dry season, while Mokao will remain at the encampment to welcome visitors expected to stop off on their way to the weekly market at Intawella, some fifteen kilometers west of the encampment. Mowa draws near the group, carrying on her head a calabash full of fresh milk, which she sets down with great care in a small hollow dug in the sand. Mokao takes a swallow and then hands the calabash to Amee, who takes a long, satisfying swallow and passes it to Bango. The calabash is passed around until the milk is finished.

It is now nearing mid-morning. The sun shines more directly down on the encampment, and it is beginning to get hot. Bango and Amee get up, put their sandals and hats back on, sling their swords over their shoulders, and leave, their arms resting on the shepherd's staffs they carry across their shoulders. Each staff is made of a straight branch more than a meter long, stripped of its bark and burnished, through long use, to a beautiful dark-brown sheen.

Amee limps because of an accident that happened about ten years earlier. He was pulled into a well by the force of a snapped pulley rope that wrapped itself around one leg, and fell some twenty meters. The leg was broken and healed shorter than the other. But Amee makes up for this handicap through his courage and cleverness.

Mowa now begins to construct a new, smaller shelter next to a bush not far from her *suudu*. She uses the flexible branches of a shrub, tying them together with small lengths of rope. She then covers this frame with mats. This small shelter, resembling an igloo in shape, will protect her from the sun and wind during the hottest hours of the day. When the shelter is finished, Mowa slips inside through its narrow opening, to be joined soon by Nebi and little Hadija.

The two women have already cleaned the calabashes

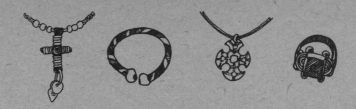

Types of jewelry given as tokens of friendship

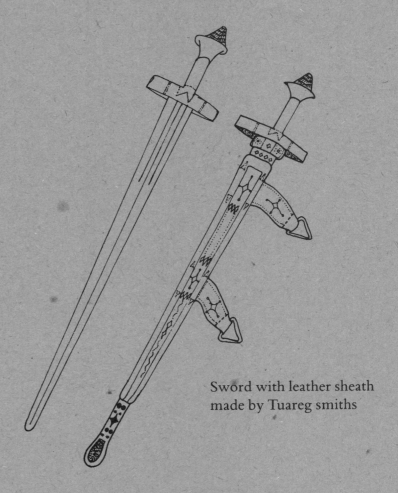

Sword with leather sheath made by Tuareg smiths

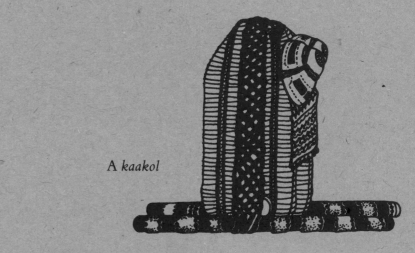

A *kaakol*

An *elletel*

used that morning. They wiped out any remaining food, scrubbed them carefully with water and sand, using bark from the *dibeehi* tree (*Acacia laeta*), then rinsed them with water. With the tip of an index finger, they then rubbed the engraved band on the outside of the receptacle with curdled milk to give the design a paler color.

One of the calabashes is in need of repair. With an awl, Mowa bores holes along each side of the break, then laces a palm fiber through the holes and pulls it tight to draw the edges together. Meanwhile, Nebi tends to her infant daughter. At least until the age of two, children are the object of constant attention. An infant accompanies its mother everywhere—whether on her back, wrapped in a cloth, or placed next to her on a mat—and is nursed on demand.

Two women—Tuwa and Fatiima—from a neighboring encampment, about ten minutes' walk away, come to join the little group. Fatiima carries with her a piece of blue material, bought at market, from which she will fashion, and embroider, a long sleeveless tunic for her husband, Boka. Tuwa is going to make a round calabash cover; for this she has with her a bunch of dried fronds of the doum palm, some dyed red, some black, some green, some left their natural straw color. After cutting them into thin strips, she softens them by soaking them in water, and weaves them together. The women talk while working. Tuwa, who has just spent hours pounding millet for the evening meal, complains about pains in her back.

"There's no end," she sighs as she deftly intertwines the strips. "When I finish this, I have to go and gather wood for the fire."

"And I have to make a bark blanket for my donkey," continues Fatiima in the same vein. "As you say, there's no end to it. If only we could rest when we get old! And the men say we are but *jom-suudu*, mistresses of the home!"

Mowa, the eldest, says nothing, but she is not without thoughts on the subject. She would complain not of an excess of work but of her dependence on the men of the encampment, in particular, although she is very much attached to him, her husband. She must follow him wherever he goes and obey his orders but must never be seen in close physical proximity to him. She has no role in the important decisions concerning life in the encampment, the herds, or relations with other families. And since she had to leave her own family to live in her husband's encampment, she still does not really feel at home but maintains a discreet and respectful attitude toward the in-laws on whom she is dependent.

Granted, a small share of the herd of cattle is hers in her own right. But she is not free to do anything she likes with her cows. She may not, for instance, sell them in the market. She may sell any milk and butter that have not been consumed by her family, which gives her a little pocket money. "In short," Mowa thinks, "the only things I really own here are my calabashes and my *kaakol* and *elletel*. They are the only things I could take with me if I ever left Mokao."

Nebi, too, is silent. She is sad. Her marriage to Bango was a marriage of choice, and she knows that soon Bango will take another wife, the one chosen for him by his father when he was only seven years old and his fiancée an infant. Nebi is afraid of not getting along with the newcomer. Besides, she loves Bango and cannot bear the idea of having a rival.

In the polygamous society of the Wodaabe, the basic union is the *koobgal* marriage, arranged by parents within a single lineage, preferably between the children of brothers or cousins. The couple are betrothed practically from birth. Marriage rituals follow, stretching over many years, but the pair are considered really married only after the wife has set up her *suudu*.

A man may choose a second, a third, and even a fourth wife, from another lineage. These choices are entirely free. Such marriages (called *teegal*), given the element of free choice, imply for their part a deeper sentimental attachment. The system establishes a certain balance between *koobgal* marriages, parentally imposed and uniting members of a single lineage, and *teegal* marriages, based on personal choice and uniting people of different lineages.

When Nebi met Bango, three years earlier, she was already married according to the *koobgal* ritual. They met during the rainy season, in the middle of the most beautiful ceremony of all, the *geerewol*, a reunion of her lineage, the bii Korony'en, and Bango's, the Kasawsawa. At night, beneath a star-strewn sky washed by the light of a pale moon, young male Kasawsawa were dancing in a circle. Bango was among them, his face painted in yellow and white, his lips blackened, and the long lines of his silhouette accentuated by the airy grace of an ostrich plume. Nebi, wearing her most beautiful embroidered wrapper, had come with her sisters-in-law to admire the dancers, and was immediately struck by Bango's beauty.

From the circle of dancing men, Bango had noticed her among the female spectators surrounding the dancers and had winked at her several times to show his interest. Nebi responded by lowering her eyes. Bango left the dance, went to her side, and they exchanged a few words. During the following days they met again on several occasions, having to be satisfied with private conversations. Then, one night, they stole off into the bush, far from the eyes of others.

The following year, again during a *geerewol*, Bango arrived on camel back near Nebi's encampment. At nightfall, he gave the agreed-upon signal, imitating a male goat's bleating. On the pretext of feeling ill, Nebi slipped out of the bed she shared with her husband and went to join her lover. Bango took her straight back to his encampment. His brothers were waiting for them. Laabon, the eldest, slaughtered a ram; the meat was divided and grilled over the fire. During this time, Nebi was waiting in the bush; she could neither attend the meal nor eat any meat, although by this *teegal* ritual she had become Bango's wife.

Immediately after Nebi's flight, the abandoned husband had tried to get his wife back. First he had lodged a complaint with the council of elders, who see to it that the rules of discipline and reciprocity are respected. They went to see Bango and tried in vain to convince him that he should give Nebi up.

For several days Nebi continued to sleep in the bush to the east of Bango's encampment, and he would join her at night. Then, gradually, she drew nearer the encampment. During this period, her father came looking for her three times in a row to take her home with him. The fourth time, Nebi decided formally to remain Bango's wife. One year later, little Hadija was born of this union.

The harmattan begins to blow, raising clouds of sand and dust. To protect himself from the grains of sand, which sting his eyes and cheeks, Mokao wraps his head in a turban nearly five meters long. He settles down on a mat in the shadow of an acacia tree to await his visitors. To pass the time, Mokao is making a rope that will be used to bind the donkeys' legs during the night. He uses fibers from the doum palm, which he has softened in water. He twists them together, pulling tightly and incorporating new fibers into the twist to lengthen it. To keep the rope in place he puts the loop at the end of it around the big toe of his right foot. As he works, Mokao thinks about his herd—his riches, his chief reason for living, his source of joy and prestige. Without it, he could not provide for his family's needs and he would lose his independence.

For the Wodaabe, devoted exclusively to animal husbandry, their livestock is the guarantee not only of material security but also of social standing. Above all they have a personal attachment to their zebus. Each is named after its mother and is given a nickname based on its physical appearance.

Mokao has about twenty cows (of which only four are producing milk), ten oxen, and two bulls. He also has thirty-five goats and sheep, which serve as bartering currency at market and can be slaughtered to provide meat for special occasions, and two donkeys for transporting baggage and water. The Wodaabe do not consume goat's milk in any form.

Maintaining the welfare of the herd during the dry season is an exhausting task for the men: pastures are ever rarer and the water level sinks lower and lower in the wells. "The women don't spare themselves, either," Mokao thinks. "Some work even harder than men."

Mowa, for example, Mokao's wife of about five years, is known by all for her energy and capacity for hard work. Before she became Mokao's wife, Mowa had been married three times. She left her first two husbands and, as tradition demanded, the sons she had with them. The sons she had with her third husband, who died, set up their own encampment. Mowa remained unattached and was living in her parents' encampment with her only daughter, Nebi, when she met Mokao. He made numerous long treks to see Mowa, staying for long periods of time in the effort to persuade her to become his wife. Several times Mowa left her family and started on the three-day trek with Mokao to his encampment but midway had a change of heart and returned home by herself. Mokao persisted for months until Mowa finally consented. At the time, Mokao already had a wife, the young and pretty Yidaka, with whom he had been united in a *koobgal* marriage arranged by his parents. Nonetheless he was taken with Mowa, though she was ten years older than he, because of her charm and thoughtfulness. Yidaka had no choice but to accept Mowa's presence.

When a man has several wives, each has her own *suudu*, her own milk cows, and her own activities. But co-spouses rarely get along well. Older wives are jealous of younger ones, childless wives jealous of those who have children. The *koobgal* wife, chosen by the husband's family from within their lineage, is theoretically the most highly regarded. This does not mean, however, that she envies the *teegal* wives any the less, chosen as they are by the husband himself and almost always out of love.

In the face of this complex situation, an attitude of restraint is called for. The most important quality for a Wodaabe woman to possess is *munyal*—patience in the face of work, fatigue, suffering, the presence of co-wives, and the secondary place that women occupy in relation to men. Yidaka was doubtless lacking in *munyal*. She was jealous and could not tolerate the arrival of this intruder, Mowa, years older than Mokao and herself. Pregnant, she returned to her mother's *suudu* to give birth. But her son died when a few months old, and Yidaka refused to return to Mokao's encampment.

Since then, Mokao has lived only with Mowa, whom he loves deeply, but from whom he has given up hope of having children. He would like to marry again to ensure himself offspring, but he knows Mowa will never accept a rival. Mokao's father, Gao. has already advised him several times to get Yidaka back. The two men have even argued about it. Gao cannot forgive Mokao for having lost the wife he chose for him. But Mokao does not want to risk losing Mowa, who remains his favorite.

However, the presence of children in a Wodaabe family is of prime importance. Not only do they help their parents with the daily chores; they also take care of them in their old age. "A couple without children is like a tree without fruit, and will be alone until death," say the Wodaabe. They prefer to have boys, for boys stay in the encampment all their lives, while girls leave to follow their husbands and thus often end up far from their parents. Aged parents always live with their sons and depend on them for their subsistence. Indeed, the Wodaabe have a system of preinheritance: throughout their lives, on the occasion of births and marriages, parents give their children part of what they own, most often animals. Consequently, when they get old, parents possess practically nothing. A possible solution to Mokao's dilemma, his worries about having a son, would be adopting a child of a relative. Mokao would undertake the child's upbringing and treat him as his own son.

Aladin, the sand-colored Saluki who guards both the encampment and the herd, begins to bark furiously. Mokao lifts his head and looks to the west of the encampment, where tradition prescribes that visitors present themselves. Three silhouettes appear in the vaporous early afternoon light as if out of nowhere; the men, perched atop their camels, seem to float in the air.

They have halted now, and say: "*Assalam aleekum* (Peace be with you)."

They wait for Mokao to come to meet them. He instantly gets to his feet and, following tradition, takes with him neither his herder's staff nor his sword, as proof to the newly arrived guests that he has no hostile feelings toward them. While approaching them, he says several times, "*On jabbaama, on jabbaama* (Welcome, welcome)."

Once he is standing before the three men, who remain perched on their camels, Mokao reaches out with his hand to touch theirs, without looking at them; and says, "*Foo modon, foo modon* (Hello, hello). *E dum onon* (It is you)."

The visitors then make their camels kneel, and they dismount. On the ground, they squat facing Mokao, who squats too. They exchange lengthy formal greetings. Mokao addresses each of the men in turn, and each in

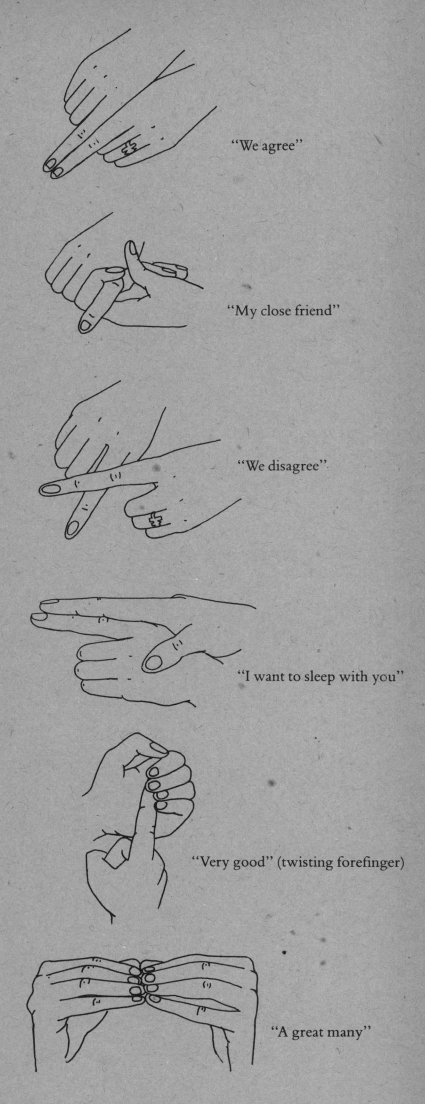

"We agree"

"My close friend"

"We disagree"

"I want to sleep with you"

"Very good" (twisting forefinger)

"A great many"

Hand gestures used by Wodaabe in conversation

turn replies. The dialogue continues for more than a quarter of an hour, and ends with the following exchange:

"*Barka* (Be blessed). You have understood well," says Mokao. And they answer: "*Barka* (Be blessed). You have understood well."

The visitors then say to Mokao, "Rise! Stand up."

He immediately obeys, and says, "Come, draw near, welcome."

One of the visitors answers, with great reserve, "No, we are fine here."

Nevertheless, leading their camels, the guests follow Mokao, who guides them toward a spot of shade a bit apart from the encampment. They remove the camels' saddles, laying them on the sand, and bind the animals' forelegs with short ropes, while Mokao sweeps the sand with a handful of dry grass to remove twigs and thorns. Nebi brings the visitors mats on which to sit, and Mowa sets a calabash of milk and a bowl of water before them. Each of the guests drinks a little milk. Tradition requires that a visitor, if not a close relative, take very little of what is offered him.

While Mokao prepares tea, his brothers go off discreetly to slaughter a ram, which is done in the dry season only on special occasions such as this. A guest must be warmly welcomed. First of all, it is a question of basic reciprocity among people who lead the same harsh and difficult life in a hostile environment. The survival of all depends upon this. Further, it is necessary to anticipate a guest's every desire, for "he brings good fortune, friendship, and peace." "One must converse with him, feed him, offer him drink," and, above all, as Mokao says, "open one's heart." To be good, speech must "come from the heart and not from the mouth."

The conversation begins in earnest. It bears first on the climate, which, for Mokao and his visitors—Jani, Dimoun, and Berto—as for all Wodaabe, is of primary importance. Their activities are ordered and their lives lived by its rhythms. So it is in this period of *dabbunde* (December–January), when the days are sunny and warm, nights are cold, and there may even be frost.

"The cold is bad," says Jani after taking a swallow of water. "It has killed a child in the bii Korony'en lineage."

"Yes, the *dabbunde* is hard living," remarks Dimoun, next to him. "Happily, we are back in our *ngenndi*."

The *ngenndi* is the area to which each group of families are most attached. They spend the long months of the dry season there awaiting the return of the rains, staying as near as possible to a well. Since the great drought of 1973–74, certain members of the encampment have been choosing this difficult period to leave temporarily for the villages to make enough money to buy some animals and millet. Some go even farther, to neighboring countries. Most Wodaabe deplore this behavior, which seems unworthy of a true nomad.

Berto, the eldest of the visitors, does not mince words. "They say still more men and women from the bii Hamma'en lineage have left their encampments for the villages," he mutters. "Everyone knows what they do there: the men work as night watchmen and the women sell themselves for money."

"What's more, they eat badly, grow weak, and fall sick," declares Jani. "It is a disgrace."

"And it has been this way since the great drought," remarks Dimoun darkly. "You remember how much suffering there was in all hearts. Men died, women died, children died, death was everywhere. And there is no greater misfortune than death, for there is no remedy against it."

"Yes, death is a great misfortune," Berto continues in the same vein, "but the greatest misfortune is the death of cows. There were men who went mad because their cows had died. I know one who lost his entire herd. He gathered all the horns and skeletons in the middle of his encampment and began to call his cows by their names as if they were still alive."

"And others," Dimoun adds, "went from encampment to encampment asking, 'Have you seen my cows?,' when they knew quite well they were dead. And the answer given was always, 'Yes, yes, I saw them. They're over there, a bit farther away. . . .'"

"Besides, they are doing all they can to make us change our way of life," says Berto, sounding more and more pessimistic. "I hear they want to force our children to go to school. That's not where they'll learn to saddle a camel!"

"But soon there will be no more camels," Dimoun declares. "Ever since they opened their new highway over there, the one that goes from Agadez to Tahoua, their truckers drive through every night like madmen and kill our animals. One of my cousins lost two zebus that way the other week."

"As for me, my camel died too, but of old age," says Mokao. "I'm going to have to go to the market to buy another."

"Go, like us, to the Intawella market," Jani advises. "There are fine animals to be had there, and they're not too expensive."

At this moment, Laabon, Mokao's elder brother, brings a large wooden bowl containing pieces of grilled mutton, and Jae, another brother, places the ram's head, skin, hooves, and tail on a mat. Berto asks Mokao for an empty calabash, and Mokao has Mowa bring one. Then Mokao and Mowa withdraw. The visitors divide the pieces of meat, distributing them between the two calabashes. They call Mokao back, give him one of the calabashes, which Mokao goes to offer his family, and set to eating the contents of their own. Once their meal is over, Mokao rejoins them.

Jani looks at the sky, where the sun still shines, surrounded by a yellowish halo, and announces: "It is time to leave." The three men saddle their camels, and, drawing them by the reins, move off toward the west. Mokao accompanies them.

As they walk, the three visitors keep repeating, "*Mi yetti on. On barkidi.* (I thank you. May you be blessed)."

Mokao answers:

"*Sey yeeso!* (Until another time).

"May Allah be with you during your journey and may Allah see you home in good health.

"Greet your family.

"Greet the people of your encampment.

"Greet your cousins and friends.

"Greet the members of your lineage."

Jani, Dimoun, and Berto remount their camels and make them stand up. They take with them the ram's head, skin, hooves, and tail, which they will show to those they encounter on their way, saying, "Look what Mokao gave us. He welcomed us warmly. May he be blessed."

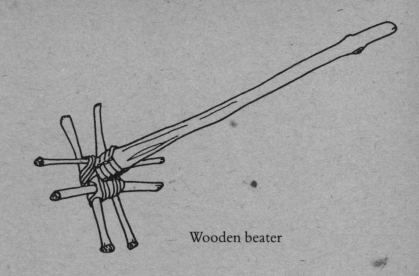

Wooden beater

While Mokao was entertaining his visitors, Mowa did not stop working for an instant. As soon as her friends Tuwa and Fatiima returned to their encampments, Mowa took the milk remaining from the morning's milking and poured it into a special calabash having a tight lid. Then, seated on a stool, she shook the calabash back and forth to separate the fat from the milk. Soon clumps of butter appeared on the surface. As she worked, Mowa scooped them out with a ladle and placed them in a smaller calabash. Then she beat the remaining milk, using a stick with four shorter pieces of wood tied to one end, which she twirled between her palms. The beaten milk, *pendidam*, with all the fat removed, is smooth and thick like yogurt, and sour.

Mowa now pours some millet into a wooden mortar; she dampens the millet with a little water and begins to pound it. The pestle is so large and heavy that she has to hold it with both hands. She pounds in a regular cadence, producing a dull, rhythmic sound. It is an exhausting task, especially in the heat of the day, and it calluses her hands and strains her back. As each batch is completed, she separates the bran from the flour, using a round sieve. Then she pours more millet into the mortar and begins the whole process anew.

Looking up from her work, Mowa sees an immense pinkish-brown smudge forming on the horizon. Bit by bit it encroaches on the blue sky and advances in her direction. Once again the wind comes up; a sandstorm is near. Mokao comes running to collect the empty calabashes used by the visitors. He brings the mats, which he has already picked up, to his wife's *suudu* and helps her cover her table with them. They hastily lash

everything down as the gusts of wind pick up force. In the now ocher-yellow light, sky and earth merge. In a few instants, the sand erases all traces of human and animal life. Mokao and Mowa sit on the ground, backs to the wind, waiting for the storm to pass. After about half an hour the cloud of sand moves off and the sky grows clear again.

As soon as the sandstorm has passed, Mowa rekindles her fire by adding a few dry branches, and above it she sets a metal tripod, blackened through use, on which she places a cast-iron pot. She pours in some water and millet flour and prepares the *nyiiri*, or porridge. At the end of the cooking time, she adds more millet flour, beating it in with a large wooden spatula. *Nyiiri* is the most frequently prepared millet dish.

Consumption of milk and of millet varies, depending on the season. During the rainy season, milk is abundant and is the staple of the Wodaabe diet. During the dry season, the lack of milk is made up for by millet dishes and sometimes by rice, wheat, or sorghum cooked in water. All these cereals are bought by the Wodaabe at the market.

Mowa has hardly finished making her *nyiiri* when Bango and Amee return. They have driven the herd home from the well, where they spent the day. They join Mokao and settle in next to him. Mokao calls to Mowa: "*Aan, worroy!* (You, come here!)." Mowa immediately brings them a small calabash of *pendidam* with a spoon. The brothers sit in a circle around the calabash and eat in silence, passing the spoon counterclockwise.

Mokao does not call his wife by name because it is forbidden to do so. Tradition not only forbids husbands to call their wives by name but also forbids parents to address by name the first two children born to them. The prohibition of the use of names applies to children in their relations with their parents and to couples and their in-laws. "What you love," the Wodaabe say in explanation of such restrictions, "you respect, and therefore you do not show that you love it. You do not express your feelings or the interest you have in someone." Thus couples may show no signs of affection in public, and the same applies to parents and children.

It is the fear of *semteende*, or shame, that enforces tradition and that explains the extreme reserve, *pulaaku*, that the Wodaabe observe constantly among themselves and in the most ordinary acts of daily life. This reserve extends even to the way they look at things. The Wodaabe say, "The eyes are afraid of what they see, especially of what they see for the first time." This is why a Bodaado never stares. He will not stare at an object or person, for he is afraid of feeling ashamed. "If you look at something, it is because you want it, and then you are ashamed."

Stemming from this all-pervasive fear of *semteende* is a spirit of mutual aid, for a poor man is ashamed and shames those around him. If, then, a Bodaado finds himself impoverished, he will be given money to buy millet or will be given milk, a cow, a goat, a sheep—whatever it takes to avert the shame of being poor. Thus, the bond that unites all Wodaabe and causes them to say that "without mutual help, there is only death," is due not only to friendship and to the spirit of collective survival. It also springs from the will to avoid shame.

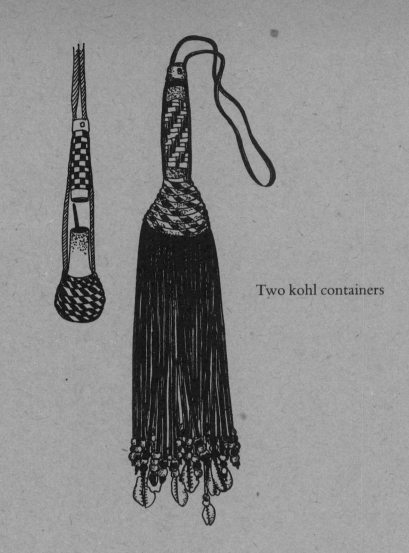

Two kohl containers

It is the end of the afternoon. Following the sandstorm, the sky has cleared. The light, which all day long has been rather hazy, has again become crisp and clear. Mokao and his two brothers stretch out on their mats. They are soon joined by their cousins Agola and Boka, sons of two of Mokao's uncles. Boka is dark-skinned and rather short, but his radiant smile and jovial manner gain him the attention he craves. Agola is the same age as Mokao and Boka, that is, about thirty. He attaches great importance to his appearance. Besides the traditional sheepskin *dedo*, he wears a long pale-green tunic and a deeper-green turban. Several times a day he accentuates his eyes by putting antimony powder (kohl) along the edge of his lower eyelids. This is a common practice among Wodaabe men. Agola has a good sense of humor and is very charming. He has a sociable disposition and likes to be surrounded by his cousins and friends.

In conversation among cousins of the same age, *waldeebe*, no holds are barred. They tease one another in a lively and outspoken fashion, not sparing references to *semmbe* (virility, strength). They make fun of themselves

and of others in graphic terms, often comparing one another to animals. One has the nose of a bull or of a toad, another the ears of an elephant, a third the mouth of an ostrich or of a donkey. Shortcomings of character are also criticized: "He's as stupid as a hyena," or "He's as wicked as a serpent."

This evening Agola is in a particularly playful mood. His first target is Boka. "You, Boka," he says, "how does your wife manage to find you in the night? Your skin is as black as charcoal!"

Boka is not slow with his rejoinder: "And you, Agola, everyone knows that, like a sheep, you have no *semmbe*. How do you manage to please your wives with your 'thorn'?"

"The 'thorn's' size has nothing to do with the case," Agola replies. "What counts is what you do with it. And *togu* counts even more. I saw you eyeing Mariyama today at the well. She didn't even look at you."

"Rest easy," Boka assures him. "She'll look at me when I dance. And I'm the one who will take her off into the bush. Not you!"

"Unless we take her together!" Agola retorts.

Indeed, the *waldeebe* are closer than brothers because they belong to the same age group and from childhood have shared the same games and activities. They are very free not only among themselves but also with women. Sometimes it happens that two or three will slip off into the bush for a rendezvous with the same woman, whom they share.

While the men joke together and relax, Mowa and Nebi continue to work. Mowa heads into the bush to gather wood. Nebi, watching her daughter play with the dog Aladin, is embroidering the tunic Bango will wear for the dances of the next rainy season. She uses brightly colored red, yellow, white, and green thread bought at the market, stitching them into geometric patterns after designs learned from her mother.

Neither woman would ever think of questioning the fact that they work while the men rest. The men are *jom-wuro*, masters of the encampment. Responsibility for the herds lies with them: choice of pasture, watering them at the wells or ponds, treatment of illnesses, choice of itinerary for the migrations. The bush is the men's domain—everything lying beyond the calf rope, that is, everything lying outside the women's domain. But a man's workday does not have the regular rhythm of a woman's. While she remains tied throughout the year to the daily tasks allotted to her, a man's activities and responsibilities vary with the seasons. Nor do men spend every day tending their herds. They can have their brothers or sons replace them if, for example, they want to welcome guests, visit a neighboring encampment, or go to market. In addition, when the day's work with the herd is done, they have some free time, which they spend braiding ropes or making necklaces and talismans, all the while chatting together and drinking tea in the shade of a tree.

The sun is now very low on the horizon and will in a few minutes disappear with startling suddenness. But it still will not be pitch dark; the sky will remain light for some time.

Boka and Agola get up, stretch, and leave for their own encampment. Mowa is still working. She has finished the evening milking of the cows. She puts the cast-iron pot over the fire, and now prepares a sauce to go with the millet porridge. She pounds together balls of peanut paste, dried tomatoes, gumbo, herbs, and a bit of salt, then adds a little water and cooks this mixture, thickening it with millet flour. Using volcanic rock as a flint, Mokao has lighted a large fire a short distance to the west of the *suudu*. Before lighting the fire, he placed some crushed leaves of the *barkehi*, the good-luck tree (*Piliostigma reticulatum*), on the spot as a talisman to ensure the fertility of the cattle. The fire (*dudal*) symbolizes the cattle's prosperity. It serves as a beacon for the herds of zebus during the night.

When Mowa finishes making her sauce, she covers it with a stream of melted butter and pours it over the *nyiiri*, which she has divided into parts, since men, women, and children eat separately, in groups according to age. The men's portion is placed in a black wooden

bowl decorated with silver studs reserved for their use. Mowa brings it and some fresh milk to her husband and his brothers. First they eat the millet porridge with its sauce. When the sauce is finished, Mokao pours some milk over the remaining porridge and mixes it all with a wooden spoon.

Night has fallen. Mokao and his two brothers leave, making their way on foot toward Boka's encampment. The stars, the moon, and the small fires of the scattered encampments are their only guides. When they arrive, they find Boka seated on a mat in the company of Hasan and Huseyni, his two brothers. On a mat on the other side of the fire is Altine, their father. After the customary greetings, the guests sit down on Boka's mat, facing Altine, who remains somewhat apart owing to his age: a father does not usually sit on the same mat as his sons. Moreover, Altine is one of the elders, the *ndotti'en*, to whom the *mbodangaaku* tradition is entrusted.

Although a *ndottiijo*, Altine remains very active. But above all he is the "wise man" to whom one goes for advice and guidance. He will remain the head of the family to the end of his days, even though he has delegated certain of his powers to Boka, his eldest son.

Nonetheless, his grandchildren can be very free with him. No taboos hamper this privileged relation. For example, if Altine playfully asks his granddaughter Haliima if she would have him as her husband, the child teases him in return: "You're too old! You have a scratchy beard! You don't have enough milk cows anymore! How can I marry you?"

The children adore Altine because he tells wonderful stories. They crowd around him, the fire's darting flames lighting up their eager faces. The night is cold, but everyone is wrapped up in blankets, and all hands are stretched toward the fire. From now until bedtime is the best part of the day for the Wodaabe, the hour when everyone talks, laughs, tells stories.

Tonight old Altine has promised to tell the children two legends about the origins of the Wodaabe. Altine has learned these stories through the oral tradition: he heard them from his own grandfather, who in turn heard them from his.

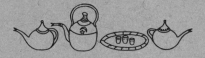

In reality, no one knows the origin of the Wodaabe people, a subgroup of the Fulani.

Certain anthropologists, basing their theory on Fulani legends of an origin in the Orient, maintain that the Fulani represent an intermixture of Jews and Africans. Thus the Fulani would be the descendants of Egyptian Jews who were persecuted by the Romans and fled Egypt. Others, basing their theory on the fact that Dravidian languages have a morphology close to that of

Rock painting from a Tassili cave, Algeria, dating 4000–2000 B.C., with features typical of Wodaabe encampments

the Fulani, have observed a similarity between the Fulani and Persian nomads and believe that the Fulani came from Iran.

The most generally accepted theory of the Fulani's origin is that they come from Ethiopia. The hypothesis is that they occupied all of northern Africa before the arrival of the Berbers, that is, approximately 3000 B.C. In 1860, Heinrich Barth, the famous German geographer and one of the earliest great explorers of Africa, posited a migration of the Fulani's ancestors across the central Sahara. This migration was confirmed a century later by rock paintings discovered by the French archaeologist Henri Lhote. Research carried out in the desert has, indeed, provided much new information on the great epic of the Fulani.

Since 1960, Lhote and other archaeologists working in the Sahara and notably in the Algerian Tassili have found thousands of rock paintings representing cattle. Their discoveries indicate that at a certain time the Sahara was fertile and inhabited by herdsmen. These herdsmen bear an astonishing resemblance to present-day nomadic Fulani: they have the same elongated silhouette; their long hair and braids are very similar to those of nomadic Fulani of today; the clothing of both men and women is nearly identical; the cattle in these paintings have lyre-shaped horns, like those of the cattle

of contemporary nomadic Fulani; and, finally, there is the same layout of the encampments and shelters, the same calf rope. There are also Negroid figures in these paintings. The herdsmen seem to have lived in symbiosis with them, and this is still the case. The nomadic Fulani depend on neighboring sedentary peoples for the fabrication of tools, clothing, and jewelry, as well as for the supply of millet.

These herdsman ancestors of the Fulani would have lived in the Sahara between 4000 and 2000 B.C. and ranged its central region, passing through north Tibesti, Tassili, Hoggar, and Adrar des Iforas. But the desertification of the Sahara, which began in the second millennium B.C., forced the Fulani to migrate to the west to find grazing lands for their herds.

In the eighth century A.D., we find the Fulani where Senegal is situated today. They then spread out over the whole of western Africa. For six or seven hundred years they were to recognize no central authority. But at the end of the eighteenth century a Fulani chief, Osman Dan Fodio, called Sheefu by the Wodaabe, and for them a legendary being endowed with magical powers, converted to Islam and enlisted a large segment of the Fulani into an army to spread his religion. In this way, at the beginning of the nineteenth century he built a powerful Muslim empire. Upon his death, in 1817, his empire split in two. The western half was entrusted to his son Abdullaahi, and the eastern half to his son Bello, who made his capital in Sokoto, in what is now Nigeria.

The eastern Muslim empire survived until the arrival of the British in Nigeria at the end of the nineteenth century. The success of the jihad, the holy war led by Osman Dan Fodio, created among the Fulani an elite that is still powerful. The families belonging to the Toroobe clan, for example, have acquired land, houses, and slaves. They have become detached from the traditional nomadic Fulani way of life, settling down and intermarrying with other groups. Many other Fulani have settled in the villages and for the most part renounced the nomadic life. They live, rather poorly, mostly from agriculture, but some still raise cattle—not the long-horned zebus of the Wodaabe but a short-horned breed. They are called Fulbe by the Wodaabe. Of the Fulani who have remained nomads, the Wodaabe of Niger are the main group. Numbering between 40,000 and 50,000, they no longer make up more than a minority within the 6 million Fulani in Africa.

In the beginning of the twentieth century Wodaabe herdsmen began to arrive in Niger in successive waves. They fled both the constraints imposed on them by the Muslim chiefs and the colonial penetration of Nigeria by England beginning in 1880. Their herds were terribly reduced following the drought of 1890. Each group charted a separate course, some heading toward Filingué, others toward Dakoro, still others toward Tahoua or In Gall, and they have remained in these areas.

The Wodaabe group is made up of two clans, the Degereeji and the Alijam. They claim descent from ancestors named Degereejo and Ali, two brothers, of whom Degereejo is believed to have been older. In the course of time, each of the sons of Degereejo and the sons of Ali formed his own lineage. Some of these lineages have as many as 1,000 to 5,000 members. Because of their large size, the lineages have themselves been divided into sublineages.

Many Wodaabe have attachments or family in Nigeria. The elders all still remember the old capital, Sokoto, and it has a place in their oral tradition.

Before beginning to speak, Altine removes his turban, uncovering his close-cropped white hair; he lies down on his side, propped up on one elbow, and after a look around at the silently watching assemblage, he embarks on his story, speaking in a low, tremulous voice.

"What I am going to tell, my eyes have not seen, but my ears have heard it from my grandfather.

"Two orphans, Fu and his sister, slept every night before a great fire, near a river. One night, a cow came out of the river, drew near them, and then withdrew. The next day the orphans moved their fire farther from the river bank. This time a vast herd appeared, drawn by the flames mounting to the sky. But frightened by the presence of the two children, the herd returned to the river. On the third day, Fu and his sister lit their fire still farther away from the river. Once more the herd approached the fire. This time the animals grew accustomed to the orphans' company, so much so that when the children left the river, the herd followed them. Fu and his sister married and had two sons: the first was the ancestor of the Fulbe, the second of the Wodaabe. When they were grown up, they divided the herd, the elder brother choosing the cows with the short horns, and the younger those with the long horns."

Altine falls silent. The fire, on which Mokao has just thrown some dry branches, crackles. A cow's muted lowing is drowned out by the sound of a camel noisily ruminating. Altine has closed his eyes. His wrinkled face reflects the light of the flames. The children hold their breath. Is it over already? Will Altine tell any more stories tonight? Yes! His eyes open again. "That is not the only legend recounting our people's origins," he says. "Here is another."

"Addam and his wife Addama had many children but could not feed them. One day Addam's father, Anabawa, told him that he must light a fire during the night at the seashore, and that with patience his problems would be solved. Following his father's advice, Addam went to the ocean, lit a fire, and waited. After a while a cow and a bull emerged from the water, but upon seeing Addam took fright and returned to the sea.

"The next morning Addam explained to his father what had happened the night before. Anabawa then gave him a talisman to put into the fire. At nightfall, Addam returned to the seashore, lit a new fire, threw in the talisman given him by his father, and waited. A bull and a cow appeared out of the sea, and this time they were not afraid of Addam. Addam led them into the bush. In the morning Anabawa gave his son a calabash and a rope to tie up the calves who were going to be born, and explained to him how to milk cows. Henceforth Addam and Addama were able to feed their children, the ancestors of the Wodaabe."

Altine is silent again. Then after a moment he adds:

"There are many other legends. But tonight I have spoken enough."

Wodaabe families move through the seasons over hundreds of kilometers of the inhospitable Sahelian steppe in search of water and grazing for their animals—sheep and goats, donkeys, camels, and, above all, zebu cattle, whose milk is the mainstay of their diet. During the dry season, from October to June, these nomads endure extremes of heat and cold and searing sandstorms as they move from place to place with all their possessions.

In their encampments each wife sets up a shelter (*suudu*) of thorny branches—roofless and roughly semicircular—within which are placed her bed, table, ceremonial calabashes, mats, and cooking utensils, including a mortar and pestle used for the pounding of millet, the cereal that supplements the Wodaabe diet of milk in various forms. While the women preside over the *suudu*, milk the cows, cook, and care for the children, the men carry out the laborious tasks of grazing and watering the animals. Yet they always have time for camaraderie and for welcoming guests in accordance with Wodaabe tradition.

Calabashes are important in both the daily and the ceremonial life of Wodaabe women. Only a few are used as utensils, to hold milk and millet porridge. A newborn baby (its pigmentation still underdeveloped) is traditionally bathed in a calabash.

The greater number of calabashes, treasured as ceremonial possessions, constitute a woman's riches and source of prestige. They are given constant care and attention, carved with elaborate designs passed down from generation to generation, and protected in woven baskets.

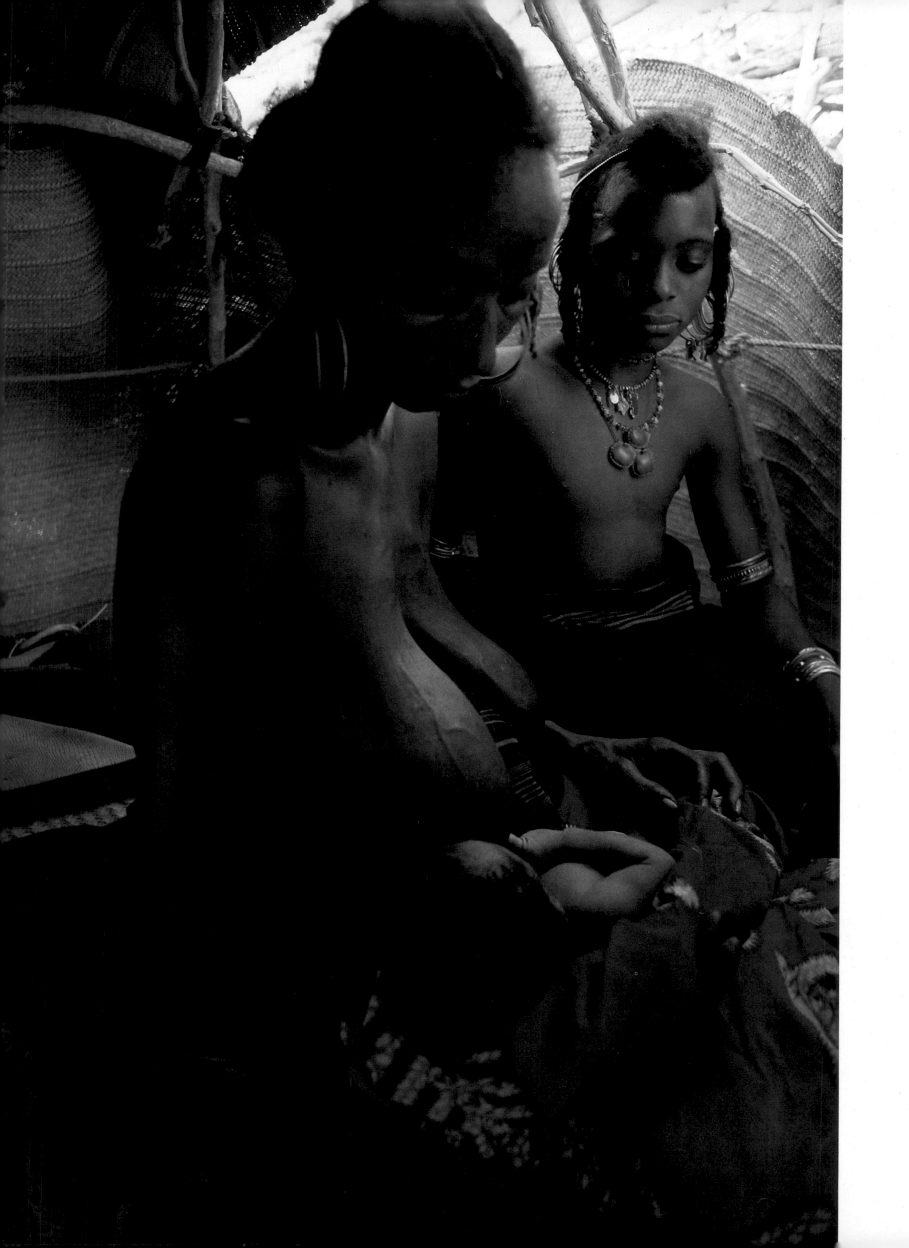

Wodaabe children are much loved, but tradition severely restrains parents from openly expressing love for the first- and second-born. Adoring uncles and grandmothers provide additional tenderness.

Free of care, Wodaabe children imitate the dancing of their older brothers, substituting long stalks of grass for ostrich-plume headdresses.

The three glasses of sweetened tea that Wodaabe men prepare and drink periodically throughout the day provide both relaxation and energy—and inspire the imitation of children.

Wodaabe can be identified by hair styles, patterns of scarification, and the talismans they wear. To scarify, small cuts are made with a razor blade and covered with charcoal; on healing they leave a dark-blue pattern of fine raised lines. During babyhood a traditional fan-shaped pattern is worked at the corners of the mouth; as a child grows, geometric designs are added below the temples, on the forehead, and alongside the nose.

Hairdressing is done by women. Traditionally, they arrange their own hair in two side braids, with a third braid twisted into a knot on the forehead and a fourth knotted on the nape of the neck. Men's hair is arranged in four thick braids, two on each side of the head, and from ten to fifteen thinner braids on the nape of the neck.

Wodaabe believe that certain roots, leaves, grasses, and barks have magic powers. These are crushed and encased in small leather pouches that serve as talismans, which are worn in the hair, around the neck, across the chest, and on the elbows. Benefits to the wearer are thought to include greater attractiveness to women, increased beauty and charm, heightened virility, and protection against sorcerers, swords, and evil spirits. Talismans may even bestow invisibility upon a young lover on the prowl.

Most family relationships among Wodaabe are restrained, in accordance with the tradition of reserve (*pulaaku*). However, among male cousins of the same age (*waldeebe*) all prohibitions are lifted. *Waldeebe* may openly display affection toward one another, and they playfully do battle over women (whom, in fact, they sometimes share).

Hospitality is important in Wodaabe life; guests must be generously welcomed, for it is believed that they bring happiness and honor. Wodaabe try to anticipate their guests' desires, offering tea and milk and often slaughtering and roasting a sheep or goat as a sign of esteem.

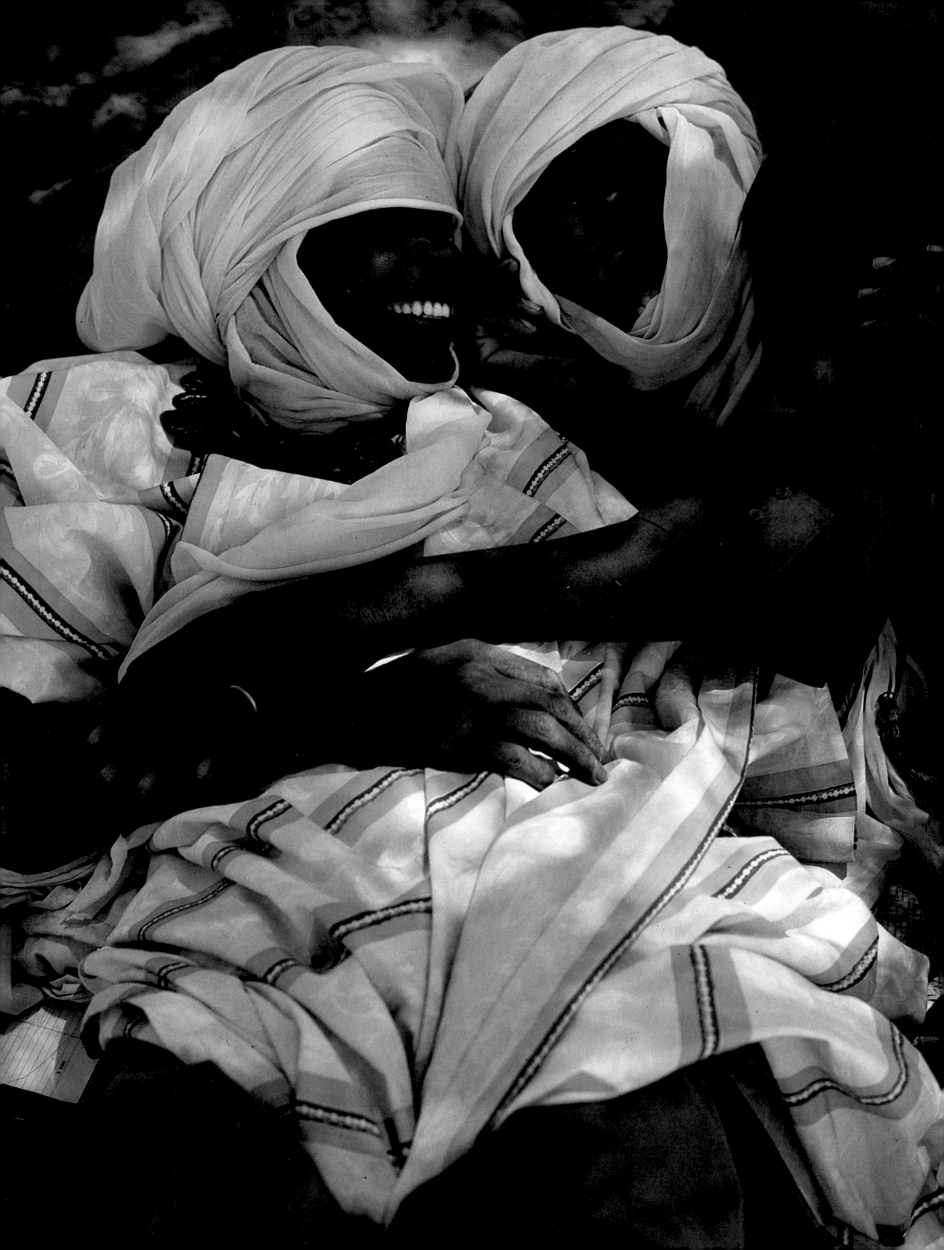

AT EGGO WELL

During the long months of the dry season, wells constitute the only source of water for men and animals, and it is near a well that each group of families set up their encampment. The well's environs become their *ngenndi*, their home base. But every three to four weeks the Wodaabe must break camp to seek fresh pastures. In this fashion they keep moving their encampments farther away from their home well.

Eggo Well, forty meters deep, was commissioned by Mokao's grandfather and built by Hausa well diggers more than fifty years ago and has remained the property of the Kasawsawa lineage. Each year in the dry season about three hundred people live within its orbit. Such wells are the collective property of the families who commission their construction, and their use is strictly reserved to the group that has had them dug. When their own wells are empty, it happens at times that the Wodaabe draw water at Tuareg wells. This sparks arguments, which are sometimes limited merely to exchanges of insults (flung as often by women as by men), but which also on occasion develop into fights in earnest, at sword point, leading to injuries and even to deaths.

In contrast to the traditional wells, like Eggo Well, which can be up to fifty meters deep, there are shallow wells, only four to five meters in depth. These are deep holes dug by the Wodaabe themselves in dry stream beds. The walls of the hole are shored up with branches to keep sand from falling back in. A shallow well belongs to the two people who dig it, and from one dry season to the next it has to be newly cleared because in the meantime it has filled up again with sand.

Mokao and his brothers Laabon, Amee, and Jae are leading their herds to Eggo Well, as they do every second day. Today Bango has stayed in the encampment to care for a sick cow. Mokao walks ahead, his braids hanging down from under the brim of his hat. He holds his shepherd's staff in his right hand; in his left hand he holds a coil of heavy rope, as well as an empty goatskin bucket with which he will draw water from the well. He advances unhurriedly, from time to time urging his animals on with the traditional herdsman's call, "*Heuii. . . . Heuii yahe he heuii yahe. . . .*"

The animals immediately close ranks, lowing as they continue on their march. Their hundreds of hooves treading the sand raise clouds of dust. Whenever an undisciplined animal threatens to stray from the procession, Mokao raps him on the horns with his staff to make him rejoin the herd.

The zebu (*Bos indicus*) of the Wodaabe is of the Bororoji breed. It is probably of Asian origin. Despite numerous crossbreedings through the centuries, the Wodaabe's zebus bear a strong resemblance to those found in Bouthan, in northern India.

The herd's composition is carefully managed by the Wodaabe. The ideal is to have as many milk cows as possible, to provide for day-to-day food needs; a few oxen, which can be sold at market; a pack ox (of the more docile Azawak breed); one or two stud bulls; and a few young bulls, some of which will be sacrificed on the occasion of important ceremonies. To govern the whole herd and lead it during migrations, a cow with a dominating character and natural authority over the rest of the herd is chosen. Bororoji cows are renowned for their discipline and sense of direction.

Milk cows represent the real wealth of the herd. If a man does not have milk cows enough to provide for his family's subsistence, he is lent one by a friend. The borrowed cow, called *habbanaae*, is brought to the borrower on a Sunday, the herd's lucky day. On the following Sunday the borrower and his family walk to the lender's encampment to thank him and to tie some bark fibers from the lucky *barkehi* tree to his calf rope as a sign of friendship and gratitude.

The *habbanaae* is left with the borrower until its third

OPPOSITE: A herdsman makes sure that a zebu drinks its fill.

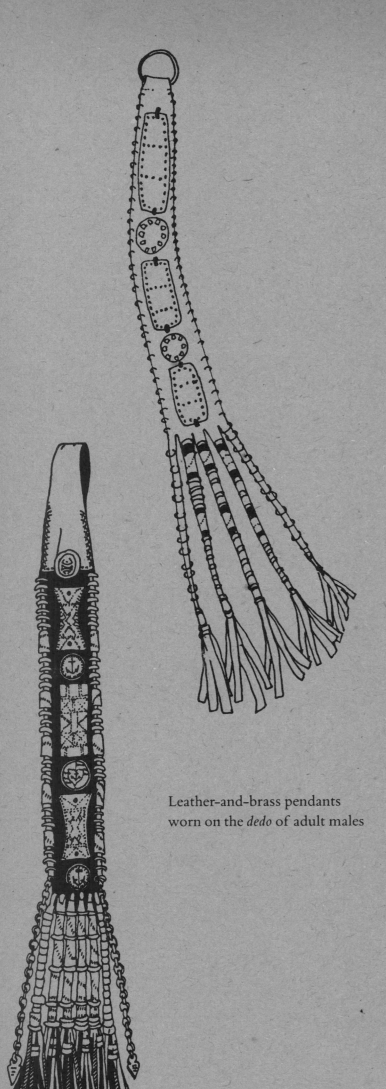

Leather-and-brass pendants
worn on the *dedo* of adult males

calf is weaned, and the borrower will remain the owner
of the three calves. This borrowed cow will be even
better treated than the other animals, since it is a symbol
of friendship. It is caressed and is brought first to the
well, and it has the right to enter the family shelter. And
it is the borrower's duty to give the owner regular news
of his cow. When its third calf is weaned, the cow is
returned to the lender, along with a heifer. In this way
the ties of friendship between the two men and their
families are maintained.

Following the herds of zebus come Jae's son, Gado,
and Laabon's sons, Belti and Baashi. Little boys are very
proud of their responsibilities as shepherds, which win
them, at the age of seven, their first *dedo*, symbolizing
their entry into the male world. On this occasion, their
father also nominally gives them their first cow.

At about the age of twelve they become *sukaabe* and
are allowed to "enter the dance." At the same time that
they learn to dance they learn the rules of justice, respect
(especially toward old people and married women), and
courtesy. These are happy years for the *sukaabe*. One of
their main occupations is to appear as handsome as
possible and attract young girls. The *sukaabe* are divided
into age groups, whose number depends on the size of
the sublineage.

The *sukaabe* elect a chief, the *samri*, with the approval
of the council of elders and of the *ardo*, the head of the
sublineage. The *samri*'s role is especially important at
the time of the rainy season celebrations, the *worso* and
the *geerewol*, when he provides liaison among the *sukaabe*,
the *ardo*, and the *ndotti'en* and is responsible for the
organization of the dances.

Around the age of forty, when a *suka* has children of
the age "to enter the dance," he presents himself,
wearing a stubbly beard and with his head shaved,
before the council of elders, bearing on his shoulder a
branch from the lucky *barkehi* tree. From then on he can
participate in the council's debates. It goes without
saying that the *sukaabe* delay as long as possible their
transition to the class of elders, for this marks the end of
the time of dances.

On the way to the well Mowa and Nebi follow
behind the young shepherds and the goats and sheep
they are in charge of. Nebi carries her daughter, Hadija,
wrapped to her back. The two women are accompanied
by Dulel, Jae's wife, and her twelve-year-old daughter,
Mogoggo. All four make the trip on donkey back, each
wearing a calabash as a kind of makeshift hat. Empty
goatskins, to be filled at the well, are tied under the
donkeys' bellies; they have been smeared with butter to

make them more watertight. The calabashes will be used to ladle the water into the goatskins.

Mogoggo is a *surbaajo*. She entered the group of *surbaabe* when she was eleven years old, and she will belong to it until the birth of her first child. Mogoggo has long been "promised," according to the *koobgal* marriage ritual, to the young Bello.

A *surbaajo* can participate in the dances and enjoys complete sexual liberty. During the rainy season celebrations she dresses with great care and wears much jewelry. The *surbaabe* are governed by one of their older members, who in turn receives her orders from the *samri*, the *sukaabe*'s chief.

After the birth of her first child Mogoggo will enter the class of married women and will be called *yeriijo*. There is no ritual to mark this transition. She will henceforth, like her mother, Dulel, and like Mowa, have to devote herself entirely to her family and to the duties that are her lot as a married woman.

Midway to the well the animals come across a few thorny acacia shrubs and clumps of dry grass. These are meager fare, but in this season anything that can be swallowed lessens the feeling of hunger. The zebus, followed by the donkeys, nibble the grasses. The goats and sheep cluster around the shrubs, devouring the lower branches. The camels ridden by Gao and Altine, enjoying the advantage of their height, tear the higher branches from the shrubs, chewing them as they proceed to the well.

Soon the well comes into view. But what Mokao sees first is the horde of animals and men crowding around it. Herds from other encampments have, in fact, preceded them. The throng is, however, in no way disorderly. On the contrary, each herd has taken its place in a star formation around the well, where the first to arrive work frantically to water their animals and fill their buckets.

"We're going to have a long wait," says Mokao. "Let's go sit down in the shade of those bushes." He heads off, followed by Amee. Soon they are joined by Boka and Agola.

While awaiting their turn, the women sit off to one side and tend their infants and watch the children playing nearby. Some of the children break branches off trees and gather pointed stones to make into bows and arrows; others caper about in the sand.

Early childhood is a privileged time. During their first years, *bibbe* (children) are allowed by their mothers to do whatever they like. They are free to discover the universe surrounding them, as well as their own bodies, at their own pace. The Wodaabe begin to impose disci-

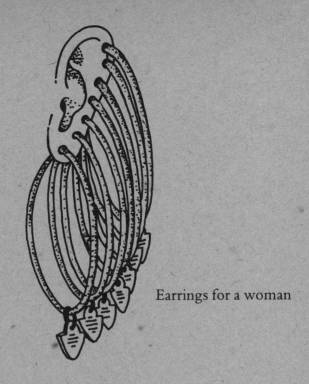

Earrings for a woman

pline on children and teach them the first rules of their moral code from the age of five.

From a very early age a Wodaabe child's education inculcates a sense of responsibility at the same time that it develops independence. Girls help their mothers carry out the daily chores in the encampment, while the boys are being introduced to the shepherd's vocation. Children, both boys and girls, perform numerous small services in day-to-day life, and often act as messengers. Their chores take up a few hours of the day. The rest of the time they play together.

Between the ages of two and four, a little girl's ears are pierced and she begins wearing small earrings; by the time she is grown, she will wear seven to ten large earrings in each ear. A little boy's left ear is pierced (among the Wodaabe the left side is the male side) for an earring that he will wear until he turns seven. Between the ages of three and eight, boys are unceremoniously circumcised, usually by a Hausa, who travels from one encampment to another throughout the dry season.

High-spirited, active, resourceful, imaginative, and creative, Wodaabe children seldom seem unhappy and are rarely to be seen crying. When they do cry, their parents generally ignore it, so that they soon become discouraged and stop. In the evening they go to sleep whenever they like. They often play, dance, and sing until late in the night.

Mowa and Dulel watch the men toiling around the well. "They work hard, you have to admit," says Mowa.

"Yes, so long as there is water," Dulel replies scornfully, "but when the drought truly sets in, they go to pieces, the poor men. They don't know what to do with themselves. Not like us."

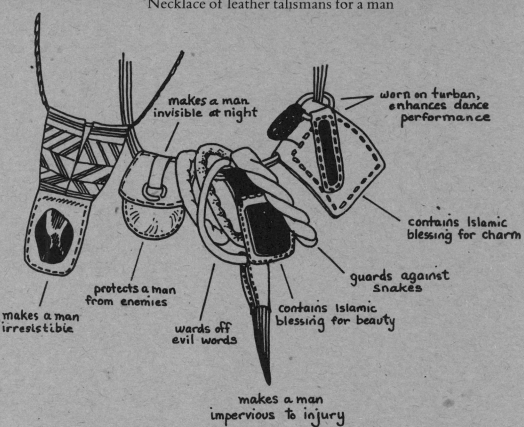

Necklace of leather talismans for a man

makes a man invisible at night

worn on turban, enhances dance performance

contains Islamic blessing for charm

protects a man from enemies

guards against snakes

makes a man irresistible

wards off evil words

contains Islamic blessing for beauty

makes a man impervious to injury

"It's true that we get along better when things go badly," Mowa acknowledges. "I remember the time when I went to the villages to dress Hausa women's hair to earn a little money."

"And I, to repair their calabashes!" Dulel adds in the same vein. "And crush their millet! And Beyoode, taking her little girl, Kannde, with her, left Laabon and went to work for several months weaving mats in a village in order to be able to take a little millet back to the encampment. Yes, all in all, we are braver than the men! They would rather die in the bush with their animals than look for a way to survive."

"There are some who do try," Mowa remarks. "Look at Agola! He went to market to sell remedies."

"Granted," Dulel answers. "But there are not many like him."

"Well," Mowa says with a sigh, "let's hope this dry season will not be as hard as the last ones."

Seated in the shade of a bush, Agola takes advantage of the enforced wait to make talismans. From a small leather bag he takes various powders made from tree barks and crushed plants, each kind wrapped up in a scrap of cloth, as well as two tiny glass bottles containing other bits of bark impregnated with perfume. He lays all this out on a mat, next to a piece of leather, an awl, a knife, and a roll of thread. He cuts the leather into strips and pierces holes in them with his awl. Each strip is made into a small pouch. Into each one he puts a mixture of powders, barks, and perfumes according to magical recipes that he keeps a jealously guarded secret.

Finally he strings the pouches together with a thin leather cord, by means of which he can carry the talismans around his neck.

"When did you begin to make these talismans and remedies?" asks Amee, observing Agola with some curiosity.

Agola smiles, somewhat bitterly.

"You remember the year of the great drought," he says, "when our herds were dying of hunger and thirst. I had only two cows left, and there I was with my mother, my brothers, and my wife, who was swollen. I hadn't a single bull left to slaughter to give a name to the expected child, not an ox I could sell to buy millet to feed my family."

Mokao and Amee nod their heads in silence. They have known similar trials.

"So I thought about it," Agola continues, "and I remembered what my father had taught me before he died. He had shown me plants and trees and had explained to me how to make preparations to attract women, to fight headaches, to resist the influence of sorcerers. . . . He told me everything. That is when I went into the bush and looked for these plants and tree barks."

"Which plants and trees?" Amee asks, still curious.

"You don't expect me to reveal my secrets!" Agola replies. "I gathered all the plants and all the barks and crushed them and went to the village to sell these remedies."

"And did they work?" Mokao asks.

"Very well," Agola answers, "so well that I was astonished. I first sold a powder to cleanse the stomach. I told the people that they must dissolve it in water and drink it. They did so, and when they saw that it worked, they came to ask me for more. Then I found other remedies. One day a man came to me and told me he could do nothing with his wife. So, I returned to the bush. I cut some roots pointing toward the sky, the roots of a tree knocked down by the wind. I mixed these roots with others, crushed them, and added some hot pimento and soda. I returned to the village and gave this remedy to the man, telling him to eat it with some meat."

"And what happened?" Amee asks.

"Well, he took the remedy and, come nightfall, his 'thing' stayed straight like the roots pointing toward the sky until the morning. So, he went to tell all the others: 'It's fantastic, the remedy is good!' And a few days later, other men came to find me. I sold and sold this remedy. And I still sell it." With a teasing smile, he adds, "If you want some, I'm ready to sell it to you."

The Wodaabe believe strongly in the effectiveness of their talismans and traditional remedies, which are prepared following recipes passed from father to son and are part of the inheritance of a lineage. They extract a perfume from the leaves of the *sotoore* tree (*Tapinanthus globiferus*) and from the resin of the *badaadi* tree (*Commiphora africana*). They fight the influence of sorcerers by washing their bodies with water containing the crushed bark of the *tanni* tree (*Balanites aegyptiaca*). They protect themselves against their enemies with the aid of an ointment made from the fruit of the *barkehi* tree (*Piliostigma reticulatum*). To chase away evil spirits believed to have induced madness, they burn the pink seeds of *roogo* grass (*Manihot esculenta*) on a brazier and make the sick person inhale the smoke.

Other plant substances are used to make remedies. As an antidote for poison, they use *garahuni* leaves (*Momordica balsamina*). Crushed *gajaali* leaves (*Cymbopogon giganteus*) are taken with milk to cure venereal diseases. For snake bites, the dried, pulverized roots of *Leptadenia lancifolia* macerated in milk are applied to the punctures, and *bambambi* (*Calotropis procera*) induces vomiting, which is believed to eliminate the venom. *Eedi* leaves (*Sclerocarya birrea*) are applied to scorpion bites. *Badaadi* bark (*Commiphora africana*) is used to relieve stomach cramps, and the leaves of the *sotoore* tree (*Tapinanthus globiferus*) to soothe labor pains.

The Wodaabe pharmacopoeia is highly reputed among neighboring ethnic groups, and this is why some of the Wodaabe who leave the encampments temporarily during the dry season travel as far as Mali, Nigeria, the Ivory Coast, and even Senegal. Upon arrival in a city, they settle on the fringes of the market. After a few weeks or months, they return to their encampment with their hard-earned money.

While Agola works on his talismans, Amee, more

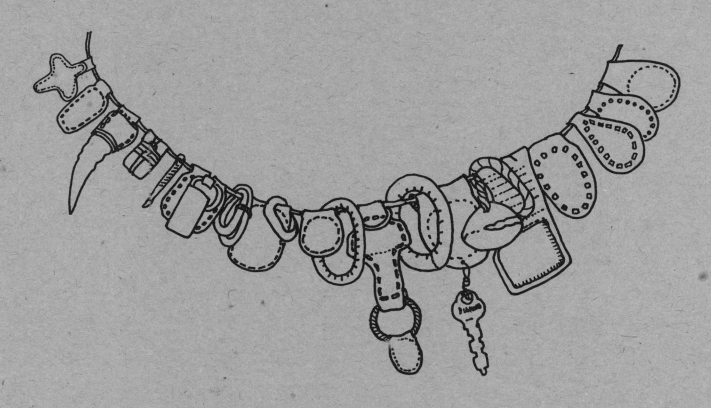

A man's necklace including talismans to increase charm

Silver picks used by women in hair-dressing and worn as hair ornaments

prosaic, spends his time working with a pair of metal tweezers to extract from the skin of his feet the tiny thorns of the dry grasses called *hebbere* (*Cenchrus biflorus*). When Amee finishes this task, he signals Gado, who comes to his side. "Go tell Hasana to come fix my hair."

Hasana, who is renowned for her deftness in dressing both men's and women's hair, arrives shortly and sits down. Amee lies down on his side and places his head in her lap. She first undertakes to undo the numerous long braids around his head. For this she uses a small silver pick with a decorated triangular head. When Amee's hair is loose, Hasana rubs butter into it to make it smoother. She then makes three parts, one in the middle and two running across Amee's head; starting from these parts, she plaits his hair into new braids, two thick ones on each side and fifteen thinner ones in back. Then she shaves the hairline above his forehead and on the nape of his neck with a razor blade.

A little distance away, Jae tries, with Laabon's help, to single out a young bull from the herd. It has become necessary to castrate the animal because it has grown skittish and has been sowing disorder in the herd. The two brothers chase the bull and manage at last to catch it. They seize it by the horns, catch its legs, turn it over on its side, and tie up its legs. Laabon grabs the animal and holds its legs in the air. Jae clamps off the testicles between two sticks, then with an ax handle beats against the upper stick, crushing the spermatic cords. Butter is rubbed on the testicles, and water is poured on the animal "to refresh its heart." When the operation is over, the bull struggles to its feet and rejoins the herd.

The Wodaabe have a vast store of traditional lore about veterinary genetics and medicine. They use time-honored methods and remedies, grounded partly in magic, to treat sick or hurt animals. Procedures include bleeding, scarification, and branding with a red-hot iron; remedies are concocted of ingredients such as plants, milk, butter, and cow dung.

Certain treatments are suggested by simple logic. If an animal has a fever, the Wodaabe splash its entire body with cool water and force it to get up and walk around to promote circulation. To deal with infection in a hoof, they shave down the base, then lance it to drain the pus. In the case of a fracture, after setting they hold the broken bone rigid with a bark splint. If a zebu has an incurable defect—a congenital malformation, albinism, or loose horns—it is not killed. The Wodaabe become too much attached to their animals for that.

The Wodaabe have practiced two kinds of vaccination since well before the arrival of the Europeans: against smallpox and against pneumonia. For the first, they introduce smallpox pus into a shallow incision made in the animal's skin with a sharp-edged stone. For the second, they let a piece of lung tissue from a cow dead of pneumonia ferment in milk. They then cut the nostril of the cow to be treated and introduce the vaccine.

However, the nomad's veterinary knowledge is gradually being lost as more and more new techniques of European origin are implemented. Cattle plague has practically disappeared since Niger's veterinary services began requiring an anti-plague vaccination.

By noon the area around the well is sufficiently clear for Mokao and his family to move up their herd. This is not a simple operation for the men or for the animals. First the animals must be regrouped and directed in the right order toward the stone troughs that ring the well.

The top two meters and the lip of the well are made of cement. Around the well opening there is a cement platform into which six forked branches are set. The well rope slides over a heavy wooden pulley threaded onto a piece of wood resting between the two prongs of each fork.

Mokao attaches one end of the rope to an ox and ties a goatskin bucket to the other. He slides the rope over the pulley and throws the bucket into the well; it falls with a dull thud. When it is full, Mokao signals little Gado to lead the ox attached to the rope away from the well. The rope gradually tautens and slowly draws the filled bucket to the well's rim.

With Amee's assistance, Mokao hoists the bucket out of the well and carries it to one of the troughs, into which he pours its contents. At once the thirsty cattle jostle one another to get to the water. Mokao strikes the horns of those advancing too fast and watches to be sure that no more than five or six are around a trough at one time. Then he returns to toss the bucket back into the well. The ox drawing the rope is again led away from the well. The rope stretches out a distance of fifty-five meters. And the bucket, full again, is pulled back up.

On the other side of the well, Agola and Boka also lug their full bucket out of the well; no sooner do they empty it into a trough than the zebus converge on it. Throwing the bucket back into the well, the men begin anew. The operation is extremely dangerous: if a wooden fork breaks, the snapped rope flying toward the well may entangle the herder and pull him into the well.

One of the troughs is surrounded by goats and sheep, watched over by the young boys. At this moment Mokao's father, Gao, and Boka's father, Altine, arrive, perched majestically atop their camels. Advancing with long strides, the camels clear a path among the little animals clamoring around their feet; spreading their forelegs apart and leaning forward, they stretch their necks, lower their heads, and noisily begin drinking.

Meanwhile, the watered herds begin to move off, lowing as they go, while others arrive and wait for their turn. The men strain to keep their animals grouped together. The plodding of oxen continues relentlessly, hour after hour, while the men, bent over double, grow ever wearier under the weight of the full dippers. It will take Mokao more than four hours to water his herd.

Only when the animals have all been watered do the men pour into the troughs the water that the women will carry back to the encampment in goatskins. They use a small calabash to ladle the water into the goatskins, which when full are tied under their donkeys' bellies. This done, the women give their infants some water to drink. Then they hastily splash water on their faces, arms, and legs and scrub one another's backs. They climb back onto their donkeys and return to the encampment, followed by the youngest shepherds with their goats and sheep.

The men are the last to leave the well. They are spent. Their hands, backs, and heads ache from the hours of pulling on the ropes and hoisting the buckets. Mokao lets out the herdsman's call "*Heuii. . . . Heuii yahe he heuii yahe. . . .*" The cattle, in response, regroup and follow their master, ranks closed tightly.

The wind has fallen, and in the clear late afternoon light the long white horns glisten as they sway to the rhythm of the march. The great herd moves off and disappears slowly into the sea of light sand, against which it stands out in relief as a long, dark mass.

During the nine-month-long dry season the Wodaabe hover on the brink of survival. Pasturage dries up and disappears; water sources are scarce. Until the precious rains return, herdsmen must water their animals at wells, to which hundreds are brought every day.

The men attach their pulleys to the well and their ropes to leather buckets, and then toss the buckets into the well. The full bucket must be lifted out of the well by a pack ox, to which the other end of the rope is attached. Filled buckets are carried to watering troughs near the well, where animals must await their turn to drink. The arduous labor of watering a herd may last up to five hours.

As the dry season progresses, the basic necessities become more and more scarce, and sometimes Wodaabe must travel fourteen or fifteen kilometers to reach water. Occasionally they share wells with other nomads— Tuareg or Bouzou.

After tossing the bucket into the well, the herdsman yanks on the rope to fill the bucket, and attaches the rope to a pack ox. When the heavy, brimming bucket reaches the surface, it is hauled to the drinking troughs, where thirsty animals push and jostle to get at the water.

While the men water the animals at
troughs or metal basins, the women fill
goatskins with water and tie them under
the bellies of their donkeys, which carry
them back to the encampment to supply
daily needs. Sated for the moment, the
animals are separated and herded back to
the encampment or out to pasture.

TO INTAWELLA MARKET

M okao has at last made up his mind to go to the Intawella market to buy a new camel. Intawella is a bush village about three hours' walk from the encampment. Mokao will go on foot; Mowa, who also has a few purchases to make, will follow her husband on donkey back.

Mokao changes his worn everyday clothing for a sky-blue tunic and a long, loose sleeveless robe (*boubou*) of the same color. With great care he wraps a white turban around his head. He then cleans his teeth, scrubbing them up and down energetically, using a bit of acacia branch with the bark peeled back at one end so that the fibers form a little brush. He also blackens the edges of his lower eyelids with kohl and darkens his lips with charcoal. Then he picks up his leather money bag, slings his sword over his shoulder, and is ready to leave.

For her part, Mowa puts a beautiful indigo-colored cloth around her everyday wrapper and covers her head with a piece of printed material folded in four. Then she rubs her large brass earrings with sand to make them shine. As soon as she is ready, she mounts her donkey and Mokao gives the signal to depart.

Walking through the bush at a good pace, Mokao does his figuring. He needs a big camel at a price not exceeding 130,000 CFA francs,[1] the amount of money he has made during the previous month selling his bark and plant remedies in Mali.

Mowa, too, has a little money: 1,000 CFA francs, made by selling butter at market. With this small sum and 200 CFA francs lent her by Nebi she would like to buy for herself, among other things, ingredients for sauces to go with the millet porridge, and for Nebi a needle and colored thread for embroidery.

En route, Mokao and Mowa are joined by Agola, elegant as always in his green *boubou*. He is leading a sheep that he plans to sell in order to buy millet, tea, and sugar. But that is not all Agola has on his mind: there will be some pretty Wodaabe girls at Intawella.

On their way to the market are several groups: Wodaabe, walking briskly along, wearing their conical hats; Tuareg camel drivers swathed in blue, their eyes fixed on the horizon; and Hausa horsemen in richly embroidered *boubou*, looking like knights of the Middle Ages. The horses of the Hausa are caparisoned with lengths of black-and-white material in striking geometric designs and are bedecked with pompoms, tassels, and elaborate leather harnesses. All head for the village, whose market, like all bush markets, is a meeting place for the various ethnic groups of the region.

Numerically the chief groups are the Hausa, the Djerma-Songhaï, the Fulani, the Tuareg, and the Béribéri. The Wodaabe have dealings chiefly with the Hausa, the Tuareg, and the sedentary Fulani groups. The Wodaabe are almost all bilingual. Besides Fulfulde, their own language, they speak the Hausa's language, which is the lingua franca of Niger, and some of them also know Tamachek, the Tuareg's language.

The Hausa, who inhabit chiefly southern Niger, are the largest group in the country, representing 56 percent of the total population of 5,400,000. They are known throughout western Africa for their ability as traders,

---

[1] In accordance with an agreement concluded between France and her former colonies in Africa, the CFA franc has a uniform value: 1 French franc (FF) = 50 CFA (Communauté Financière Africaine) francs.

The smallest CFA denomination, 5 CFA fr. (1 *dalaare*), is used as the base monetary unit. Thus, when a vendor asks "100" for a particular product he means 500 CFA francs.

OPPOSITE: A Bodaado sells traditional herbal remedies at a market to earn money to buy millet for his family during the dry season, when milk is scarce.

but they also engage in agriculture and other pursuits.

The Wodaabe feel nothing but scorn for these sedentary people, who live in houses "where one suffocates" and whose work as merchants, farmers, butchers, water carriers, and artisans they consider degrading. The Wodaabe give these "grain eaters" the pejorative nickname of Haabe (singular Kado), which they apply to all black-skinned people with short, nappy hair. This disdain is reciprocated. The Hausa say that the Wodaabe are "savages who live in poverty and don't wash" and call them Bororo, after the breed of their zebus, the Bororoji. They enjoy telling stories, such as the following, that ridicule the Wodaabe:

"A Bodaado comes to a village to visit some people. He walks through the streets with his herder's staff across his shoulders, as usual. Arriving before the door to their house, he tries to walk through the narrow entrance, which is framed by two pillars, but his staff is blocked by the two pillars and keeps him from advancing. He does not understand what is happening and repeats his fruitless efforts several times.

"The Bodaado then retraces his steps and asks the people of the village what he must do to get through this door. In answering him, the villagers assume a very serious air: 'This is a secret. We will tell you if you give us a cow in exchange.'

"The Bodaado agrees, and it is explained to him that he must turn sideways to get through the door. In this way his staff will not catch on the pillars. The surprised Bodaado then says: 'Indeed I *knew* that there must be a secret for getting through that door.' "

The mutual feelings of disdain are concealed in the daily contacts between the two peoples. But once back in the bush, the Wodaabe give free rein to their derision. They compare the Hausa to animals like the hyena or the donkey, and go so far as to say that the Haabe are not fit to belong to the human race. The most scathing remark that one Bodaado can address to another is, "You are the bastard son of a Kado."

The Tuareg constitute about 8 percent of Niger's population. For the most part nomads, camel raisers, and caravanners, they migrated from Maghreb and arrived in the seventh century in the Aïr region of northern Niger. They are organized in tribes and endogamous castes. The Tuareg's well-known nickname, "blue men," derives from the fact that the indigo dye of their turbans, which cover their faces except for the eyes, bleeds and stains their skin.

The Wodaabe have ambivalent feelings toward the Tuareg. These lords of the desert and redoubtable warriors, surrounded by mystery, inspire a certain respect; their height, their light skin, their robes, which they wear over a short tunic and balloon pants, and their indigo turbans give them an almost regal air.

However, the Wodaabe have nothing but scorn for the

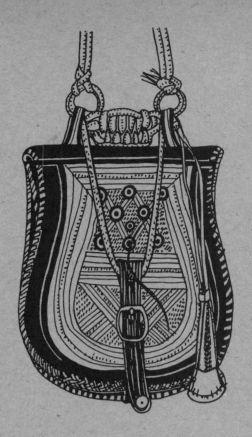

Red-and-black leather purse of a type favored by Wodaabe men

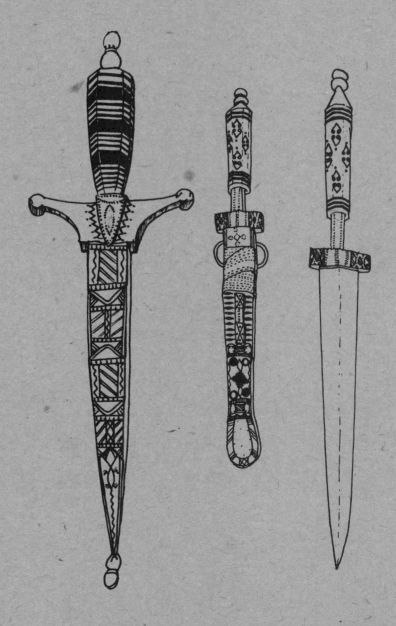

Knives and sheaths of Tuareg workmanship

former black slaves of the Tuareg who have gained their independence—the Bouzou, sometimes called Bella. Some of them migrate on their own with their sheep, goats, camels, and cattle. They are not always the owners of the animals but take care of them for Tuareg and Hausa. Others, especially the "blacksmith" caste, have settled in villages. The men work in metal, their wives in leather. The Wodaabe, while holding them in contempt, depend on them for the fabrication of swords, knives, saddles, jewelry, and leather bags, in which they are highly skilled.

At the market, the Wodaabe also encounter sedentary and seminomadic Fulani, who make up about 8.5 percent of Niger's population. The cultivation of millet is their chief means of livelihood. In addition, some raise short-horned zebus, the Azawak breed. The Wodaabe enjoy good relations with these other groups of Fulani and stress the fact that they are culturally and racially close and speak the same language, Fulfulde. But in the same breath they castigate them for having given up the traditional nomad's way of life to live like Haabe.

After three hours of walking, Mokao, Mowa, and Agola see the village of Intawella in the distance. Under the radiance of a sun already high in the sky, the blank, sand-colored walls give the city the look of a fortified citadel. But up close this illusion gives way to the reality—a maze of square ocher and gray houses and courtyards separated by narrow, sandy streets.

The village seems totally deserted. In contrast, the market set up outside the walls on its northern side is teeming with life. However, the crowd assembling there, and growing by the minute, is neither rowdy nor hurried. Buyers and sellers wander about, some on foot, leading goats, sheep, and cattle, others on donkey or camel back, with bundles of wood, sheaves of grass or straw, and other merchandise. The bursts of laughter and happy cries of this colorful and noisy throng mingle against a background of staccato drumbeats and chants sung by Tuareg women. The market is not only the place where one comes to buy and sell—taking one's time, it might be noted. It is also a meeting place where old friends keep in touch and the latest news is exchanged.

But Mokao, Mowa, and Agola have specific goals in mind. First they want to see Boubacar, a Hausa who acts as their go-between, or intermediary (*dillaaliijo*), in important transactions. The trio picks its way through the crowd, enters the village, and follows the labyrinth of narrow alleys to Boubacar's "concession," a large courtyard surrounded by a wall made of sunbaked mud-and-straw bricks. At the back of the courtyard stands a semicircular hut made of interwoven branches

and straw, where Boubacar, his wife, and his children live.

Surrounded by his family, Boubacar respectfully welcomes his visitors. Everyone sits down on mats. Water and a bowl of millet porridge are brought out, and Boubacar begins to prepare tea. Each time Mokao and Agola come to Intawella, Boubacar welcomes them and offers them food and lodging for the night. In return, they receive Boubacar at their encampment and on occasion present him with a calf.

The *dillaaliijo* takes charge of all important transactions concerning livestock, especially sales. He stands in for the seller and, as a general rule, negotiates directly with the buyer. When a seller approaches a *dillaaliijo*, he tells him the price he would like to get, for example, 20,000 CFA francs for a sheep. If the intermediary succeeds in closing the deal at that price, he will receive a commission ranging from 3 to 5 percent from the seller. But fairly often he contrives to get a higher price, say 30,000 CFA francs, and in addition to his commission he pockets the difference, without a word to his client. The buyer, too, is obliged to pay a commission to the intermediary, but this commission is fixed and represents a fairly modest sum. The intermediary also serves as interpreter. In general, he knows at least two languages beside his own, the Fulani's Fulfulde and the Tuareg's Tamachek.

Mokao, Agola, and Boubacar drink tea while talking business.

"I have a sheep to sell," Agola says. "It's not very fat, but all the same I'd like to get 18,000 CFA francs for it, because I need money to buy millet."

"Leave it to me," Boubacar volunteers.

"As for me, I'd like to buy a camel," Mokao says. "I've been told there are excellent buys to be made at Intawella. Whom should I see?"

"Go and see Idrissa," Boubacar answers. "He's the *dillaaliijo* who sells Saidou's camels, and Saidou is a well-known Tuareg camel raiser."

While this conversation is taking place, Mowa heads for the market. She is in no rush to begin making her purchases but wants to wander around and look at the merchandise for a while.

Each merchant has his spot, always the same. In the center of the market one finds merchants selling cloth, clothing, blankets, sandals, mats, calabashes, tea, tobacco, costume jewelry, beds, pottery, and dried plants and spices. All the merchants are grouped by specialty and have spread their products out on mats on the ground, protected by canopies made out of dry branches or canvas. To the east of the great expanse of sand is the livestock market, with its cattle, camels, donkeys, sheep, and goats. Nearby are feed merchants, rope-makers,

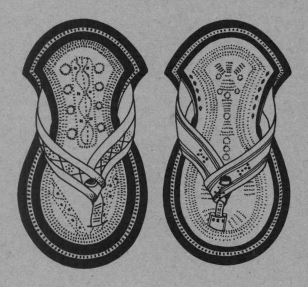

Red-and-green leather sandals made by
Hausa craftsmen

tanners, and butchers. To the west, sacks of millet and
cakes of salt are sold.

Mowa winds her way through the crowd. Suddenly
her attention is caught by a display of calabashes behind
which a Hausa is decorating one, making geometric
designs in it with an awl. He works with extraordinary
skill and rapidity, all the while haranguing the passersby.
"You want it?" he asks Mowa, holding the calabash out
to her. "I've almost finished it. It's 300."

Mowa sighs. She has never seen a calabash so beautifully decorated, but the price—1,500 CFA francs—is
much too high for her. Reluctantly she moves on and
draws near a vendor selling everything she needs for
making sauces. Set on a mat are onions in small piles,
dried tomatoes and herbs, sold by the cupful, balls of
peanut paste in packets of ten, and peanuts offered for
sale in old tomato-sauce cans.

Mowa squats down in front of the merchant and asks
him how much the peanuts are. His price, 5 CFA francs,
is the normal one, and she hands him the money. The
merchant empties one of the cans into a piece of paper
and carefully puts the can away for future use. Next
Mowa buys a pile of onions and a cupful of dried
tomatoes.

The throng continues to come and go around her.
Wodaabe men walk by in twos, holding hands. Women
do the same. There are also couples, but a man and a
woman seen holding hands are of course not married,
since a married couple may not have the slightest physical contact in public. The crowd moves slowly; people
cluster before the displays of merchandise, talk to one
another and to the vendor, trade jokes.

Suddenly Mowa finds herself face to face with Fatiima,
Boka's wife. The two women take each other by the
hand and continue their exploration together. Mowa
buys some colored thread and a needle for Nebi. Fatiima
finds, in a display of Nigerian cotton goods, a deep blue
wrapper made of woven strips sewed together and
decorated with thin yellow and red lines.

"How much?" she asks the merchant.

"500," he answers.

"That's much too expensive," Fatiima protests.

"You won't find a more beautiful one in the whole
market," declares the merchant. "Here, because you're
so pretty, I'll sell it to you for 450."

"Still too steep!" Fatiima replies. "And I see another
one that's much more beautiful over there!"

She squats down in front of another display and
points to the wrapper that tempts her. The price, 400
(2,000 CFA francs), is reasonable, and she decides to
buy it. The vendor measures the material in cubits, the
length of the forearm from the elbow to the tip of the
middle finger, cuts it, and gives it to Fatiima.

The two women now walk off in the direction of
some shops that border on the market. In their shadowy

interiors piles of goods lie covered with dust, and assortments of products are lined up on shelves. Outside the entrances Arab merchants wearing richly embroidered *boubou* are stretched out on mats, apparently indifferent to the commotion surrounding them. These are the market's big businessmen, who specialize in imported goods. Just about anything can be found in their shops: enameled bowls, cans of tomato sauce, blocks of sugar from Belgium; Algerian dates; cotton material from Nigeria and the Sudan; teapots from Libya; Tuareg fringed leather bags, swords with sheaths covered in waffled red leather, and rectangular pendent purses decorated with openwork designs.

"All this is not for us," Fatiima says wistfully. The two women turn their backs on the shops and return to the center of the market.

Meanwhile, Mokao and Boubacar (who is leading Agola's sheep) arrive at the livestock market. Tethered to wood stakes, the animals are clustered in small groups. Boubacar stops here and begins his search for a buyer for Agola's sheep.

Mokao heads for the camel market. On the way he passes in front of the enclosure where cattle are sold, mainly Azawak zebus with short, pointed horns and spotted white, black, and brown hides. But Mokao's heart tightens when nearby he sees Bororoji zebus, with their dark mahogany hides and immense horns, being sold by Wodaabe, for a Bodaado hates to part with one of his zebus. The camels are assembled in groups of about twenty, each group watched over by a *dillaaliijo*.

Finally Mokao finds his man, the intermediary Idrissa. He wears a pink *boubou* and a white turban. The lower part of his face is covered and only his keen, watchful eyes are visible. Mokao examines the camels one by one. He looks first at the teeth. If the teeth are as long as two joints of a finger, the camel is about fifteen years old—a good age. Mokao also checks the undersides of the camel's hooves to make sure that they are smooth and not swollen and have neither scales nor cracks. The length of the neck is important, for if its neck is too short the camel will not be able to walk for long distances. Above all, the camel must not be missing any toenails, for then it would not be able to run in the pebbly desert.

Mokao at last finds a camel that suits him: large, about fifteen years old, with the undersides of its hooves smooth and firm. It also has the circular patterns of long hairs on each side of its chest and on its rump that are

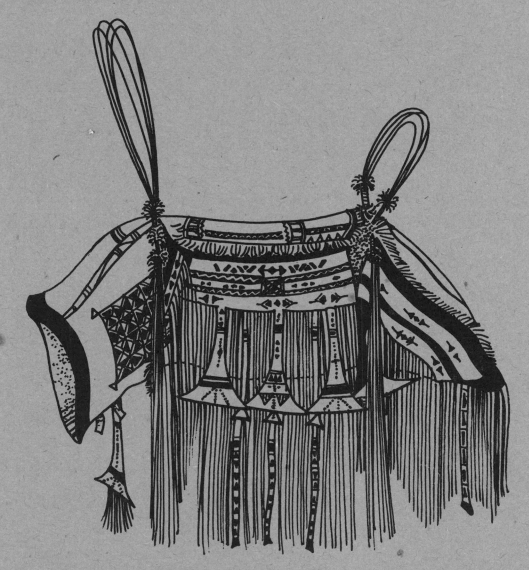

Fringed leather camel bag made by Tuareg

considered a sign of longevity.

Idrissa, sensing Mokao's interest, draws near him and begins to list, one by one, the animal's qualities. "Take a good look," he says, as he spreads the camel's lips apart to show off its teeth. Then he lifts the hooves one by one, saying, "You see, the nails are intact and the hooves have no disease; this camel will be able to run anywhere and for long periods."

"I'm not so sure," Mokao says; "his neck isn't very long."

"Maybe so," Idrissa replies, "but see how limber his back is! And look at that rump! There's all the room you could want for your wife."

He smacks the camel's rump hard, but the camel does not start. "What's more, he's very docile," Idrissa insists. "And he'll live long; look at the pattern of his hairs."

Mokao is silent. Idrissa feels that he is tempted. "He's a superb animal," he says, "and in addition, he's not dear: 34,000!"

Mokao is startled. "We'll have to talk about it," he says.

And the two men squat down.

"That's too much for me," Mokao says. "You'll have to come down."

"Out of the question. Anyone will give me that price."

"Not me," says Mokao flatly.

Idrissa shrugs his shoulders. "Well," he says, "I'm willing to lower the price by 2,000."

"That's not enough!"

"For a camel like that!" the *dillaaliijo* exclaims. "Just look at him, how handsome he is! All right! Since I know you're a friend of Boubacar, I'm willing to do a little something for you and lower the price by 3,000, but not one more."

"Still too high," Mokao says; "try again."

Idrissa throws up his hands. "Well then, how much will you give for this camel?"

"23,000."

"You must be joking! Listen, I've done my best to lower my price. You can try to raise yours some!"

"24,000."

"30,000. Last price," Idrissa counters.

Mokao shakes his head and rises to his feet. "No," he says, "I'm sure that at the Dakoro market I'll find a more beautiful animal and one that's less expensive." And he walks off.

Mokao makes his way back toward the center of the market, where there are some open-air canteens. Here Mokao espies Boubacar, who has just sold Agola's sheep. "How did it go with Idrissa?" Boubacar inquires.

"Badly," Mokao answers worriedly. "His camel is much too expensive . . . and yet it's really just what I need, that animal! But 30,000 is too much."

"Let him wait an hour or two," Boubacar advises. "I know that Idrissa is in urgent need of money. If you go back, he'll surely be inclined to lower his price some more."

Mokao shakes his head, unconvinced, then starts with surprise: Agola is passing by in the company of an exquisitely beautiful young woman.

"That Agola!" Mokao comments to Boubacar. "He already has two wives and he still has to come looking for others at the market! He's with Koki, from the bii Korony'en lineage. Maybe he wants to make another *teegal* marriage."

Not far away, Mowa and Fatiima have come to a halt before a pile of mats. They are of all sizes and from many places. Mowa is especially taken with the beauty of a splendid, very thick Tuareg mat made of reed strips woven with dark-brown leather thongs. "How long is it?" she asks the vendor.

"Three paces," he answers. This is a little over two meters—just the size that Mowa has in mind (a "pace" corresponding to a normal stride, about seventy centimeters).

"How much?" Mowa asks, more and more smitten.

"400," the merchant answers.

That's more than Mowa intends to spend. The two women turn away regretfully from the tempting display.

The time has come for Mokao to go back and resume bargaining with Idrissa. As Boubacar had predicted, he finally lowers his price to 26,000 (130,000 CFA francs), the price Mokao has had in mind. He counts out the amount, together with the usual buyer's commission of 3,000 CFA francs, and Idrissa hastens to secrete the money in his robe. Then Idrissa calls a little boy who serves as public scribe—for the two negotiators are illiterate—and has him fill out a paper serving as a bill of sale, bearing the names of seller, buyer, and intermediary, the amount of the sale, and a description of the mark of ownership on the animal. Mokao returns to Boubacar's "concession," followed docilely by his new mount.

The slanting sun, now low in the sky, sheds golden light on the animals' hides. The market begins to empty out little by little. Merchants pack their goods into large sacks, which they load onto their donkeys and camels.

Night falls very quickly now. The narrow, sandy alleyways of Intawella glow with little fires and kerosene lamps by whose light women are frying millet fritters in large pots and men are grilling mutton brochettes —both eagerly bought by passersby. The fatter the meat, the more desirable it is. From the direction of the market come muffled drumbeats, accompanied by handclapping and songs. Somewhere on the edge of the village young Wodaabe are performing a circle dance, surrounded by a crowd of spectators. Everyone feels like celebrating. Buyers and sellers alike are convinced that they have made good deals.

The scene at the market, with its buying and selling, might seem to indicate that the Wodaabe are in the normal commercial circuit and have entered consumer society. But in reality their participation in this society remains marginal. They buy and sell extremely little. Furthermore, they tend to work against normal rules of commerce because as nomads they cannot transport reserve supplies. In October, at the end of the rainy season, when the livestock are fattest and would bring the highest prices, the Wodaabe do not sell any animals because milk—the basis of their diet—is plentiful. However, this is also the time of year, after the harvest, when millet is cheap and they could purchase it advantageously. It is in April, near the end of the dry season, when the animals are thin and bring low prices, that they are obliged to sell some because milk is scarce and they need the money to buy millet—the alternate staple of their diet—at the very time when millet prices are high. Thus it might be said that the Wodaabe are as poorly adapted to commercial society as to sedentary society in general, and that here too they pay the price of their free, wandering life.

Back at the "concession," Boubacar and Mokao find Mowa, Fatiima, and Agola. All are worn out from the long day spent in the direct sun. Boubacar makes tea while his wife, surrounded by her children, prepares the evening meal. The cold begins to make itself felt. It is too late to return to the encampment; Mokao and the others will stay in their host's home and will leave at dawn.

The market has ended. Intawella drifts off to sleep.

Weekly markets such as the one at Intawella provide the opportunity to barter, buy, and sell, as well as serving as a meeting place for the Wodaabe and other ethnic groups of the region. The needs of the nomads change with the seasons. During the dry season they go to market mainly to buy millet (to compensate for the lack of milk) and to purchase buckets, blankets, and waterskins. During the rainy season they buy salt for the animals and items of adornment to wear at coming ceremonies. To pay for these basics, they sell or trade sheep, goats, and nonproductive cattle. An animal may be exchanged for an expensive object such as a sword or a camel saddle.

Wodaabe women sell curdled milk and butter in order to buy calabashes, clothing, spices, and cereals. Traditionally the economy of the Wodaabe depended on barter and exchange; they have learned to buy and sell.

The market is divided into several parts. To one side, salt and millet and other cereals are sold. To the other side is the livestock market, with cattle, camels, donkeys, sheep, and goats. In the center is the merchandise section—a myriad of stalls offering basic necessities and decorative crafts. Merchants sit for long hours, offering their goods and bargaining with the nomads, who coolly walk away if prices are too high. Both buyer and seller are adept at the waiting game.

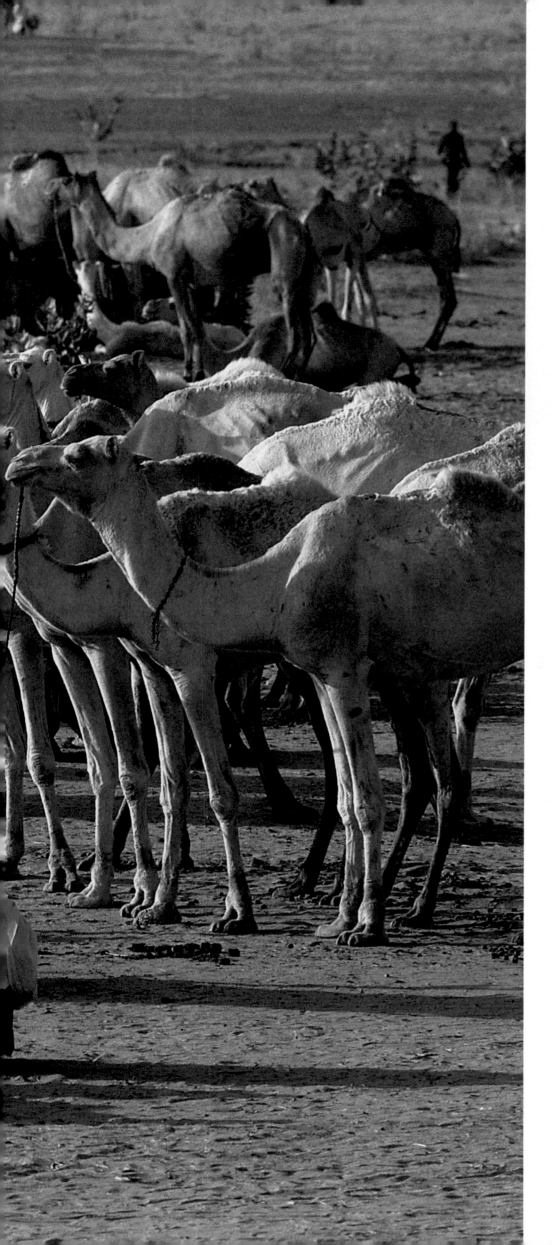

Every Wodaabe male aspires to own a camel, both for its utility and as a source of prestige, a measure of wealth. A Bodaado contemplating the purchase of a camel checks its teeth to determine its age, examines its hooves and toes, and takes special note of the length of its neck, believed to be an indication of the animal's stamina.

At the market the Wodaabe obtain a variety of goods made by craftsmen of other tribes. Among these are cowhide sandals made by the Hausa and camel saddles crafted by Tuareg. The wooden structure of the saddles is covered in red and green waffled leather and decorated with silver strips.

Hausa spice merchants offer an enormous display. Red peppers, gumbo, peanut balls, and salt are among the ingredients of the sauces that enliven the basic millet dishes of the Wodaabe.

Anticipating the rainy season ceremonies,
mothers buy heavy brass anklets for
their *surbaabe* daughters, and young
women buy earrings, beads to string
into necklaces, and bracelets and rings to
be given away as tokens of friendship.

Men buy lengths of blue ribbon (measured in cubits, from elbow to fingertip) to decorate their turbans and to make shoulder straps for their swords and purses. Women buy dark-blue hand-woven fabric to fashion into wrappers.

ON THE MOVE

ike a sail swollen with the wind, a waxen moon hangs in the starry sky, obscured at moments by an ever-increasing number of clouds. The men, gathered around a fire, glance frequently skyward. Mokao smiles. "This is good," he murmurs. "The clouds bring rain. We'll follow them."

From the other side of the fire, old Gao's voice is heard: "Don't be in too much of a hurry. The real rains are not yet with us. We must be prudent."

"And up to now, we've had mainly dry sandstorms," his neighbor Altine continues in the same vein.

"Rainstorms have perhaps already broken in the north," Agola returns.

"We'll see what Bango has to say," Gao concludes. "He shouldn't be long now."

The men look up and peer into the night, hoping to see Bango's figure emerge. All they see are the camels wandering through the acacia thickets, munching on young shoots, the donkeys strolling here and there, their long ears twitching, and the zebus stretched out on the sand, their horns catching the flickering light of the cattle's fire, the *dudal*.

As scout, Bango had left at dawn in search of new pastures and ponds large enough to water all the livestock. If his reconnoitering is successful, the great migration to the north will begin, and with it the happiest period of the Wodaabe's year, for at the end of the migration not only families but sublineages will come together after the nine long months of drought, hardship, and isolation.

A short distance away, on the other side of the bushes sheltering the goats and sheep, the women chat as they, too, cluster around a fire. Mowa, Nebi, Fatiima, and Tuwa are all busy embroidering. Little Hadija sleeps next to her mother, under the guard of the dog Aladin.

"Do you think Bango will find what we need?"

Tuwa asks as she threads a needle.

"Bango can sniff out water like a zebu!" Mowa replies. "And pastures too."

"Then we will be leaving soon!" Fatiima exclaims, delighted. As an afterthought, casting a worried eye on the work resting on her lap, she murmurs, "I'll never finish embroidering this tunic before the *worso*."

"You'll just have to keep working on it on donkey back," Mowa replies impassively.

Suddenly Aladin lets out a sharp yelp, leaps up, and tears off into the night. All heads bob up. "That must be Bango," Mokao says as he gets to his feet.

A moment later the tall silhouette of Bango perched atop his camel appears at the encampment's edge. He draws near the fire and, making his mount kneel down, slides to the ground. The men welcome him with the customary formal greetings and he makes the customary responses. Bango removes his hat, slips off his sandals, and sits down next to Mokao, holding his hands out to the crackling fire. Mowa comes to his side and sets down a calabash full of fresh milk. After taking a long drink, Bango launches into an account of his day. He had first crossed a region of hills and valleys where it had not rained for several days and as a result there was neither green grass nor water. Then, in late morning, he met a Bodaado of the bii Korony'en lineage, who received him in his encampment and, after offering him milk and millet porridge, told him where he could find abundant pasturage.

Following his directions, Bango arrived in an area of clayey soil covered with numerous varieties of grass, already beginning to wither owing to a lack of moisture. He therefore pushed on. Two hours later he arrived in the Akaddaani Valley, which had been soaked by a recent rainstorm. It was carpeted with tender green grasses. Not far away there was a pond of clear, clean water surrounded by excellent pastures.

The men have listened in silence. When Bango finishes speaking, old Gao asks the first question: "How many days' walk is it?"

OPPOSITE: Riding on a heavy-laden donkey, a Wodaabe mother and child follow the migration route.

Traditional wooden bed of a married woman

"Two days will be enough, I think."

"That's good," Altine says. "The cows must not walk too fast. They are still weak."

"And at the end of the first day," Mokao asks, "did you find a spot where we could spend the night?"

"Yes," Bango says, "near a small pond about one day's walk from here. Some Wodaabe are already camping there, but they are few, and there is pasturage enough for all our animals."

"And around the big pond, the one we'll get to the second day, are there many people there?" Laabon asks.

"I didn't see anyone," Bango answers, "but even if other encampments arrived, there would be enough water and pastures for everyone."

There is another silence while the men mull over the new information. The region Bango has discovered sounds good for the animals. What remains to be decided is the day of departure. This is not an easy decision, since for the Wodaabe there are lucky and unlucky days, depending on the position of the moon in the sky. For example, the first day of the lunar month is unlucky because the moon is barely visible. The same is true of the twenty-sixth day of the lunar month, which marks the end of the last lunar phase, when "the moon goes away." Lucky days are those when the moon is "stable." Of the days of the week, Sunday, Tuesday, Thursday, and Friday are good; the others are unfavorable. To disregard these interdictions would bring misfortune.

"We could leave tomorrow," Gao proposes. "It is a good day and what's more, the moon is stable."

After a moment's reflection, the men nod their heads in agreement. The day is well chosen; departure is set for the morrow.

"We leave tomorrow," reports Mowa, who has sharp ears, to her friends in the *suudu*. "At last. That will be a change from our life in the encampment."

"We will only have more work," Fatiima says with a faint smile. "We'll have to load and unload the pack oxen and the donkeys at the end of each leg of the

journey and walk for hours in the sun carrying calabashes of milk on our heads." She stops, seeing Mowa's face darken. "But it will be very good, all the same," she adds softly. "The cows will give more and more milk, and we won't be hungry any longer. And then soon the celebrations will begin. At last we will show off our calabashes, our *kaakol*, and our *elletel*. And we'll be together with all the Kasawsawa we haven't seen for months."

The sun has only just risen and the entire encampment —men, women, and children—bustles with activity. But this activity, although routine, is far from well-organized. In theory, all know the tasks assigned to them: Baashi, Belti, and Mogoggo must go to the pond with their goatskins for water; Gado must herd together the goats and sheep. Meanwhile Mowa and Nebi clean the calabashes used for the morning meal, nest them one inside another, and tie them up with ropes. They assemble all the kitchen utensils, disassemble the beds and the calabash table, and wrap the posts in mats.

Mowa lays a bark-fiber mat on the pack ox's back to protect it. Then, with Nebi's help, she hoists the bed and table posts, lashes them onto the animal's flanks, and, paying close attention to the balance of the load, on top of them secures the calabashes, her *kaakol*, and her *elletel*. Next, the two women set about loading the donkeys. On top of bark-fiber mats they lay their bags of millet, binding them tightly, and add the kitchen utensils, the leather sacks of clothing, the mats, and the wooden stools. Finally they hitch a goatskin half filled with water below each donkey's belly.

Everything happens in an atmosphere of the greatest agitation and of growing confusion. The herds are nervous and difficult to regroup, poorly balanced loads fall off the backs of the pack oxen, calabashes break. Men run to help the women pick everything up, upbraiding them all the while, and children, trying in their own way to be useful, are soundly scolded for their efforts. Everywhere people rush about, shout at one another, and run in all directions. Then, gradually, a semblance of order begins to establish itself.

Mokao loads his camel. He sets in place his Tuareg saddle, on which he hangs leather sacks containing his personal effects and his tea-making equipment. He drapes a striped blanket over the saddle. Then he assembles the herd of zebus in the middle of the encampment.

Around ten in the morning, the column stirs and begins to move at a slow, ponderous pace. Vultures fly in tight circles overhead, awaiting the humans' departure. Once the procession withdraws fully from the campsite, these birds of prey dive toward the ground and clean up all traces of food, while dung beetles do the same with the cow dung. In a few hours the only vestige of the encampment to attest to the nomads' passage will be the shelters' thorny branches.

The Wodaabe's migration is carefully planned. Each group of families has its own patterns and its own scouts to seek out water holes and pastures, and follows a route established by its ancestors, deviating by perhaps a few kilometers each year. Variations in itinerary from one year to the next are the result of climatic conditions: the nomads will avoid a region if it has not rained there, whether or not it is part of the traditional route. They cannot permit themselves to take chances. The survival of the herds and their own survival depends on the soundness of their decisions.

During the wet months the Wodaabe, in order to provide their herds with a balanced diet, seek out varying types of grazing land. The encampments move constantly between the hills, the plateaus, and the valleys, where different kinds of forage are to be found. During the first rains, in June, they look above all for the fresh grasses that appear with the first rains and that experience has shown are most favorable to the animals' growth and the cows' production of milk.

So as not to overtax their herds, the Wodaabe alternate days of long migration with days of rest or days in which they cover only short distances. However, they never linger very long in the same pastures, in order not to overgraze the pastures and thus do a disservice to the herders who might follow them.

Bango heads the file because he has scouted out the route. His brothers and their herds follow, advancing in parallel groups. Then come the sheep and goats, watched over by the young boys. Newborn animals are carried on donkey or camel back or even on the herdsmen's

shoulders; their anxious mothers come to check on them from time to time.

The women of the families bring up the rear. Mowa leads the pack ox loaded down with her *kaakol*. On her head she balances a heavy calabash filled with the milk remaining from the morning. She is followed by Beyoode, Laabon's wife, and Dulel, Jae's wife. Nebi, Hasana, Fatiima, and Tuwa are mounted on their donkeys, seated on top of the baggage, which they steady with their legs. The little donkeys too young to carry loads trot near their mothers. Although pregnant, Kannde, Laabon's daughter, follows on foot, wearing on her head folds of dark-blue cloth to protect her from the sun.

From high atop their camels, Altine and Gao watch the column to ensure the orderly progression of the herds and to make certain that no animal wanders off en route. The dogs of the encampments run along the length of the column, their tongues hanging out, trying to keep in the shade of the donkeys. The column advances slowly, at an average of three kilometers per hour. It is crossing a sandy, arid region where not a drop of rain has fallen for weeks. In passing, the animals crop off scattered tufts of dry grasses.

The sun is high in the sky, and the heat is punishing. Nebi dismounts, pours off a little of the water from the goatskin lashed below her donkey's belly and gives it to Hadija to drink. Approaching the head of the column, Mokao points toward some black clouds gathering on the horizon. Bango nods without saying a word: a storm is brewing. If it brings rain it will be welcome, but it may also pose some problems for the caravan. Bursts of thunder are rumbling in the distance, and long, pale flashes of lightning streak the sky.

Mokao rides back to Mowa and Nebi to help them secure their loads and cover them with mats. The wind blows harder and harder, raising clouds of yellow sand into which the bush disappears as if swallowed up by a dense fog. Then, after a series of sudden, sharp bolts of lightning, down comes the rain, in torrents. Within seconds, water soaks the dried-out earth. But this does not stop the Wodaabe; heading straight into the deluge, the column pushes onward, packed closely together, slogging through the mud.

Suddenly Mowa slips. The calabash she has been carrying on her head falls and breaks. The milk spills on the ground. The precious liquid is irrecoverable, but every piece of the calabash is carefully retrieved. Mowa will repair it at the next halting place.

Little by little the storm passes, and the rain stops almost as suddenly as it started. Steam rises from the overheated soil. The column stops briefly to let the animals water at a small, newly formed pond, then sets off again. Three hours later they reach the top of a hill overlooking the huge valley they have crossed. Gao

makes a sign for everyone to stop. The men on camel
back fan out to investigate the surroundings and to
choose the best spot for the encampment. It is quickly
decided upon: a large open sandy space far enough from
a pond to be relatively free of mosquitos, and some
distance from any trees where scorpions might lurk.

With a gesture, Mokao shows Mowa and Nebi the
place to unload their baggage and build their *suudu*. The
women first tend to the pack ox because it transports
the most precious part of the baggage. Next, they
unload the donkeys. After this, they leave in search of
trees; they chop some branches off with an ax and drag
them back to the campsite to construct a new *suudu*. In it
they arrange the bed and the table. As soon as this is
done, they go looking for dry firewood, which they
drag back to the *suudu*. They dig a shallow hole in the
sand to keep the embers from being scattered by the
wind, put some dry grass in the hole, lay the wood over
it in a star pattern, and then ignite the grass. When the
fire is going well, Mowa goes off to milk the cows,
while Nebi begins to pound millet for the evening meal.

The men have fewer chores, and within minutes of
arriving at the campsite they have unloaded their camels
and found a shade tree under which to drink tea together.

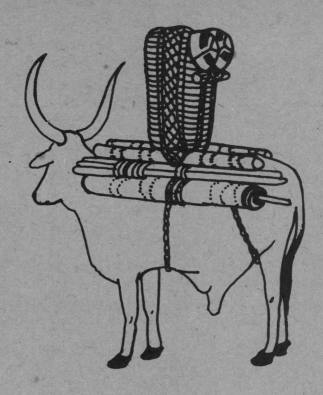

Pack ox laden with *kaakol* and wrapped bed poles

Once the evening meal is finished, the men gather
around a fire, while the women gather within the
encampment. Children come and go, playing by themselves or joining the group of their choice. The men are
in high spirits. The migration is going well. The atmosphere is joyful and relaxed, for the livestock hardly
need watching anymore but wander off alone in the
night to nearby pastures and return before dawn. And
the hour nears when tales may be told, this being
forbidden during the day.

Indeed, seizing a moment of silence, Diiye cries out:
"*Taalee, taalee.*"

To which Boka immediately answers: "*Taaleete!*"

These are the traditional words that are the necessary
preamble to the telling of tales. They invite the hearers
to listen. "If you did not say '*Taalee, taalee*,'" the Wodaabe
say, "your tale would have no head and no one would be
able to understand it."

From this moment on, all taboos are forgotten.
Anything is possible within the framework of a tale.
Even the requirements of reserve and shame—the ever-
present *pulaaku* and *semteende*—may be breached.

"Listen closely," Diiye continues, "I am going to tell
you of the animals' journey."

A satisfied murmur rises from the group.

"A camel sets off on a journey," says Diiye, "and he
meets a cow and says to her, 'I am going to drink the

water of the pond of Modoro.'"

Throughout the narration Diiye speaks the animals' lines in tones simulating the sounds the animals make—to the vast amusement of his audience.

"The cow," he continues, lowing, "answers the camel, 'I too am going to drink the water of the pond of Modoro.'

"The camel and the cow set off together, and they meet a donkey, to whom they say, 'We are going to drink the water of the pond of Modoro.' And the donkey answers, 'I too am going to drink the water of the pond of Modoro.'

"The camel and the cow and the donkey continue their journey together, and they meet a sheep, to whom they say, 'We are going to drink the water of the pond of Modoro.' And the sheep answers, 'I too am going to drink the water of the pond of Modoro.'

"The camel and the cow and the donkey and the sheep set off again, and they meet a goat, to whom they say—"

"I bet they tell him, 'We're going to drink the water of the pond of Modoro!'" Boka interjects.

"Just so," Diiye replies, "and the goat answers, 'I too am going to drink the water of the pond of Modoro.' And the camel and the cow and the donkey and the sheep and the goat set off again, and they meet a guinea fowl.'"

This time the entire assembly cries out in chorus: "And they say to her, 'We're going to drink the water of the pond of Modoro!'"

Diiye nods his approval. "And the guinea fowl answers, 'I too am going to drink the water of the pond of Modoro.' And the camel and the cow and the donkey and the sheep and the goat and the guinea fowl set off again and they meet a hen, to whom they say, 'We're going to drink the water of the pond of Modoro.' And the hen answers, 'I too am going to drink the water of the pond of Modoro.' And the camel and the cow and the donkey and the sheep and the goat and the guinea fowl and the hen set off—"

"They must be tired!" Amee cries.

"They are," Diiye returns. "Therefore, they stop. And the camel says, 'I, who have a long neck, tomorrow I shall drink the water of the pond of Modoro.' And the cow says, 'I, who have long horns, tomorrow I shall drink the water of the pond of Modoro.' And the donkey says, 'I, who have long ears, tomorrow I shall drink the water of the pond of Modoro.' And the sheep says, 'I, who have a large belly, tomorrow I shall drink the water of the pond of Modoro.' And the goat says, 'I, who have cloven hooves, tomorrow I shall drink the water of the pond of Modoro.'"

"And the guinea fowl, what does she say?" a voice asks.

"She says," Diiye answers with a cackle, "'I, who have beautiful feathers, tomorrow I shall drink the

water of the pond of Modoro.' But—"

He breaks off, scanning the faces turned toward him, and raises a cautionary finger. "And the hen?" he asks. "What do you suppose she says?"

Various answers are thrown out at once. But Diiye shakes his head. "No, the hen says, 'As for myself, I'm not going to drink the water of the pond of Modoro.' Then the guinea fowl jumps on the hen and swallows her."

Several exclamations of surprise are heard from the audience.

"They set off again," Diiye continues. "They walk and walk, and again they stop to rest. And the camel says, 'I, who have a long neck, tomorrow I shall drink the water of the pond of Modoro.' In this fashion, at each resting spot, the animals announce in turn that they will drink the water of the pond of Modoro—except the last, who is instantly swallowed up by the next to the last. The goat swallows the guinea fowl, the sheep swallows the goat, the donkey swallows the sheep. The donkey is then swallowed by the cow and the cow by the camel, who at last arrives alone at the pond of Modoro. He stretches out his neck and drinks and drinks and drinks until his stomach is filled. Then he returns to the bank and gives birth to the cow."

The listeners explode into laughter. Diiye's voice grows louder and the rhythm of his story speeds up.

"And the cow begins to drink the water of the pond of Modoro. She drinks and drinks and drinks until she gives birth to the donkey. And the donkey begins to drink, and he drinks and drinks and drinks until he gives birth to the sheep, who drinks and drinks and drinks until he gives birth to the goat, who drinks and drinks and drinks until he gives birth to the guinea fowl, who drinks and drinks and drinks until he gives birth to the hen, who drinks, and drinks, and drinks. When all the animals have drunk their fill, they return to the bush and they stop to rest in a pasture."

"Now what are they going to do?" asks Boka.

"They talk," Diiye replies. "They wonder, in fact, what they're going to do. Finally, the camel says, 'I am going to the Tuareg.' The cow says, 'I am going to the Wodaabe.' The donkey says, 'I am going to the village.' The sheep says, 'I am going to the Fulani, who raise sheep.' The goat says, 'I am going to the Bouzou.' The guinea fowl says, 'I am going to the bush.' The hen says, 'I am going to the Hausa.'"

Suddenly, Diiye stops, and in a different voice announces:

"That is the end. *Jabanannga, japtanannga, pewanannga* (Whether you accept the story or you do not accept it, the story is not true)."

All stories end in this way.

Among the women, stories are also told. This evening,

old Beyoode is the one to cry out, "*Taalee, taalee,*" and Mowa answers, "*Taaleete!*"

Beyoode begins: "The toad goes to a scorpion and says, 'Come, let us exchange blows, and we'll see which one of us can hurt the other more.'

"The scorpion answers, 'All right. Who will begin?'

"The toad says, 'I'll begin. I will hit you six times.'

"The scorpion lies down and lowers its tail. The toad gives one blow, then a second, a third, a fourth, a fifth, and a sixth blow, and the scorpion counts them aloud.

"Then it is the toad's turn to lie down. The scorpion raises its tail and strikes the toad, saying, '*Go'o* (One).'

"Immediately the toad yells: '*Jeego'o* (Six)!' and he takes flight.

"This is why the toad to this day, says '*Jeego'o, jeego'o, jeego'o.*'" Old Beyoode's pronunciation mimics a toad's croaking.

And in this way, for hours on end, tales are told among both the men and the women until very late at night.

The next morning the migration resumes. As the column moves north, the landscape changes gradually. The procession crosses a plateau of reddish, clayey soil, bordered by low cliffs. From this plateau it proceeds down to the bottom of a sandy valley, where dry river-cut channels, some up to several meters deep, meander between the terraces.

Mokao and Bango carefully examine the area, searching for the least difficult crossing points for the overburdened animals. But the donkey on which Tuwa is riding has split off from the column, determined to cross the gulley at a place of its own choosing. The result is not long in coming: the donkey skids on a sand slide, stumbles, and crashes to the ground, and the baggage flies off in all directions. Mowa and Fatiima rush to help the animal get back on its feet and to repack its load. Kannde wants to help them, but Mowa stops her: "Stay put, you with your swollen stomach. If you strain yourself, you'll be having your baby before we set up encampment again!"

When the donkey has been reloaded, the column sets off once more.

Through experience, and because they are dependent on natural resources, the Wodaabe become very familiar with the topography of the Sahel and with the characteristics of the various types of soil and vegetation. They know, for example, that in the northernmost areas of the region within which they migrate the soil provides a high concentration of salt, which is necessary for the animals' development. They have a name for each plant and tree, and know its special value as food for a particular animal. They know that during the rainy season most grasses must be consumed in their early stages of growth and flowering, for they are often harmful after bearing fruit. These grasses are extremely well adapted to the environment. Their seeds, buried in the sun-baked earth, begin to develop at the first drop of rain and sprout within a few days.

Trees are relatively scarce. The acacia is one of the most widespread of the thorny trees of the region. Several species exist: *Acacia albida*, *Acacia laeta*, *Acacia raddiana*, and *Acacia senegal* (now rare because its bark is stripped to make rope). When rains are infrequent, the roots of these trees penetrate as much as thirty meters into the ground and spread out laterally as well to find moisture. Acacia bark is thick and watertight, which limits evaporation, as does the smallness of the leaves. Triggered by a rise in temperature, the acacia's leaves bud out a few days before the first rains. In the drought these leaves wither, but they conserve some of their nutritional value for the animals that nibble them.

To their precise knowledge of their environment the Wodaabe add an astonishing visual memory of the areas they have traversed in the course of their migrations. Their nomadic and pastoral way of life, in inhospitable surroundings, has sharpened their senses and developed their faculties. Their very survival depends on this.

Moving northward through the area of recent rains, the procession advances over a blanket of grasses glistening in the sun. The herds slow down their pace to graze among the tender shoots of new grass. Mowa takes advantage of the slowing of the march to gather, in passing, a few tufts of grasses, which she will use in preparing a sauce for the evening meal. She carefully folds the cuttings into a corner of her wrapper. Nebi, riding on her donkey among the innumerable bundles, finishes embroidering the tunic her husband, Bango, will wear for the dances during the days of celebration. Despite the bumpiness of the ride, little Hadija sleeps peacefully, curled up on her mother's lap.

At the head of the column, Bango points out to Mokao a herd of gazelles grazing at a distance. The graceful animals stop short upon seeing the zebus, remain frozen for several seconds, then with electrifying speed disappear into the plain.

The Wodaabe are well acquainted with the wildlife of the region they traverse. They attribute certain good qualities and certain shortcomings to animals. Indeed they use these traits to personalize them in their tales. In a Wodaabe fable the ostrich says, "They call me the ostrich. I have two feet like the hen, a long neck like the hen, a little head like the hen, a thin beak like the hen. But what makes me superior to the hen is that she spends the night in the village, while I spend the night in the bush." This last point is a positive attribute for the Wodaabe, since they too live in the bush.

Large mammals are scarce in the region. Gazelles make fleeting appearances, and hyenas are seen on rare occasions. To the Wodaabe the gazelle—long, lean, and limber, with a light-colored hide and large eyes—is the symbol of beauty. A beautiful woman will almost always be compared to a gazelle. The hyena is the most feared of all bush animals. Its nighttime laughter terrifies. It is ugly and ill-proportioned. In tales, the worst role always falls to the hyena because it is stupid and is easily hoaxed by others. The Wodaabe avoid speaking its name aloud for fear of causing it to appear.

At dawn and dusk, numerous small animals can be seen leaving their burrows to find food: jerboas, snakes, and scorpions. Most of the snakes are poisonous, and their bite can cause death. The scorpion's bite is not fatal but can bring on a high fever and sharp pains. The Wodaabe fear these creatures and are careful to set up their encampments far from trees, tall grasses, and rocks, where they lurk. Because it is long and supple, the snake is considered handsome. But they say its wickedness far outweighs its beauty, for it attacks but does not eat its prey; it therefore represents sheer cruelty.

The Sahelian chameleon, in contrast, is not only no danger to the Wodaabe but is prized by them. This lizard of prehistoric aspect has large, bulging eyes that can move independently and skin whose color changes to blend into the surroundings. If a chameleon is killed, its body is dried and pulverized; the men mix the powder with water and coat their faces with the paste before dancing the *yaake* dance. This mixture, they believe, aids them in attracting the spectators' attention and also enables them to change color themselves, like the chameleon. The chameleon is the symbol of prudence, for it steals forward like a thief, looking all around, and camouflaging its presence through changes in color.

All Sahelian animals have mechanisms enabling them to adapt to the lack of water and the extreme temperatures. Gazelles lose relatively little water from their systems because their urine is extremely concentrated. Scorpions and reptiles, particularly the sand snake, have hard, impermeable integuments with no sweat glands. Jerboas can live without drinking, subsisting on dry plants; these little rodents sleep in their burrows, rolled up in tight balls so that the dry air they inhale gets mixed with the moist air they exhale.

Among the birds of the region are many vultures.

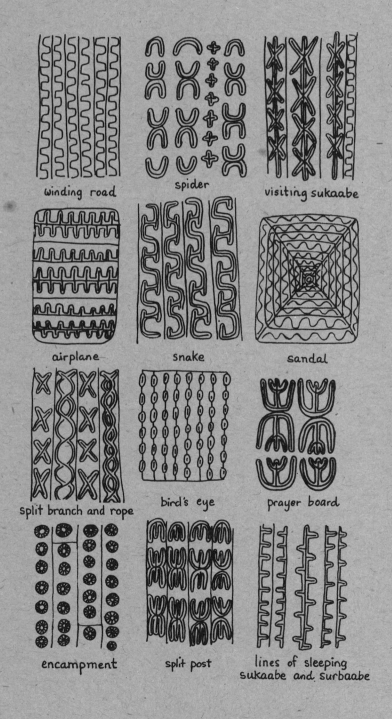

winding road spider visiting sukaabe

airplane snake sandal

split branch and rope bird's eye prayer board

encampment split post lines of sleeping sukaabe and surbaabe

Traditional embroidery designs

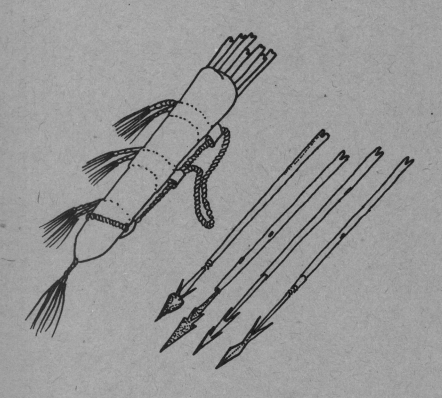

Leather quiver with metal-tipped arrows

These birds of prey glide on air currents for hours at a time in search of carrion. As soon as they spot a dead animal they swoop down on it like an arrow and tear off shreds of flesh, sometimes enormous, all the while fighting with other vultures drawn by the same prize.

Weaverbirds' nests hang from acacia branches. These little birds, very similar to sparrows, are skillful builders. They construct round nests by entwining plant fibers, straw, twigs, and grasses. Then, to stump their enemies, especially snakes, they weave a long tunnel which makes access to their nests difficult. They sometimes even build dummy nests.

Bustards are less common: strong-legged, stocky birds with long necks, who peck interminably at the ground (which they seldom leave), looking for food. Their nests are simple holes dug in the sand, and are often raided of their eggs by snakes.

Sadly, ostriches are growing more and more rare. Their plumes are highly prized by the Wodaabe, who use them to bedeck themselves for the rainy season dances. Ostrich feathers are handed down from generation to generation.

Unlike the ostrich, the cattle egret is very common. It is a small, white, long-legged bird, often to be seen on the backs of cattle, where it obtains its food—flies, horseflies, and other insects. Wodaabe quote the cattle egret as saying, "I, the cattle egret, speak: Follow those larger than yourself; do not follow your equal. For he who follows those larger will grow and have enough to eat."

Animals and birds have little to fear from the Wodaabe, for they are not hunters. The bows and arrows carried by some of the men serve only as protection against possible attacks by wild animals or against cattle thieves.

On camel back, Mokao rides down along the column of zebus to be sure that everything is in order. Suddenly his eyes flash and he is on the alert: Ole, the black cow with a long white spot on her belly, whose pregnancy is well advanced, is showing signs of nervousness. She has strayed from the herd and seems to be seeking shelter. "She must be on the verge of calving," Mokao says to himself. "I hope everything goes well." He signals his brother Amee to join him and finds the cow behind a bush. She is shaken by violent contractions. Suddenly the water breaks and the liquid floods onto the sand.

"It should go very fast now," says Amee, kneeling before Ole.

Indeed, everything does go very fast. Already the calf's hooves are appearing. With a sure gesture, Mokao grabs them, while Amee pushes on the cow's belly.

Little by little the calf emerges. Mokao lays it on the ground and blows long and steadily into its nostrils to help it breathe. The little animal begins to move its ears. Ole turns her head toward her newborn offspring and begins to lick it with long sweeps of her tongue. Soon it is totally dry.

Mokao carefully lifts the calf, whose umbilical cord Amee has just cut, and hoists it over his shoulders. Ole gets up instantly and follows Mokao to the column, where he entrusts the calf to Gao, who will carry it on his camel. Mokao mounts his own camel and leaves at a trot to rejoin Bango, who gesticulates to him excitedly. "The pond is over there!"

What Mokao sees first is a long, green mass, a real forest. Shimmers of light are visible between the tree trunks. The rhythm of the march picks up suddenly. Smelling water, the zebus hurry their pace, passing the herdsmen and breaking into a run as they weave through the trees. When Mokao and Bango finally catch up with them, they have already plunged into the pond, a sheet of now murky water in the middle of which stand some half-submerged trees. Perched on each one are hundreds of birds, raising a deafening din. The air is full of the buzzing of mosquitos and the croaking of toads. Small white butterflies flutter among the trees. Egrets, with their dazzlingly white plumage, wander along the banks of the pond. A marvelous coolness pervades the atmosphere.

The men, still atop their camels, water them without dismounting. Leaving their donkeys on the muddy bank, the women enter the water, calabashes in hand, to fill their now empty goatskins. Some take advantage of the moment to wash their faces, arms, and legs. The children too, dunk themselves in the pond. Streaming with water, they clamber back onto the bank and search for the small, sugary berries of the *tanni* tree (*Balanites aegyptiaca*); before sucking on the berries, they meticulously peel off the yellow shells in which they are encased.

Suddenly, cries and shouts come from the other side of the pond. Mokao says, "Those are bii Korony'en. I'll go see them." He urges his camel to leave off drinking and take him around the edge of the pond. A little later he returns, looking pleased. "There are pastures enough for everyone," he declares, "and I've found a good spot for the encampment."

Tuwa, Nebi, and the other women continue to fill their goatskins, calabash upon calabash, trying to siphon off only the water near the surface, where it is least muddy. The pond bottom is thick mud into which one can sink up to the knees. The Wodaabe never venture very far from the pond's edge into the water. In fact, they do not know how to swim.

After washing up, Mowa returns to the bank and gathers a large armful of *tafassa* (*Entada sudanica*) that she will cook to accompany the millet porridge of the evening meal. *Tafassa* is a green plant resembling spinach that grows in the vicinity of ponds. When the herds have been watered and the women have filled their goatskins, the herdsmen guide the column to the spot chosen for setting up the new encampment. It is an expanse of dry sand where the cracked ground bears witness to the intense drought that has just ended.

The *ndotti'en* have decided to stop for two days near the big pond. The short, tender grass is good for the animals. They will be able to regain their strength. And it is becoming increasingly obvious that Kannde is close to delivery.

Shortly before sunrise the following day Mowa is awakened by Fatiima: "Kannde is having her pains. She has gone into the bush."

Mowa and Fatiima have no trouble finding Kannde. Attended by her mother, Beyoode, Kannde is already giving birth, squatting on the ground. After receiving the baby, a boy, Beyoode hands it to Mowa, who with a knife cuts the umbilical cord to about a finger's length. Beyoode runs around excitedly, crying out, *"Ayooroorooreee! Ayooroorooreee!"* to announce the baby's arrival. Then she returns to her daughter's side and washes the baby in a calabash filled with water. The placenta is immediately buried in front of Beyoode's *suudu*, near the calf rope.

After the birth, Mowa and Fatiima help Kannde walk to Beyoode's *suudu*. They lay her on the bed and place her baby near her. They collect many leafy branches of the fragrant *faruhi* tree (*Lannea microcarpa*) and make them into a soft brush, which they bring to Kannde, along with a pot of hot water. Kannde goes behind the *suudu*. There she dips the brush into the water and beats it gently against her body to wash herself. Meanwhile Mowa and Fatiima remove any spots of blood that have fallen on the sand and bury them. Then the two women, lashing mats to a branch frame, build a small shelter to protect Kannde from curious eyes, and from the sun during the daytime.

The next day, Beyoode prepares *kunu*, a mixture of millet, milk, salt, and red pepper, for Kannde to eat, "to get the bad blood out of her." She also washes the baby and applies hot sand to the umbilical cord to dry it out. Then she massages its head, face, arms, and legs.

During the week following the birth, Kannde will not touch her baby. It is up to the women of the family to hold the baby to its mother's breast and get it to suckle. This is not from a lack of maternal love on Kannde's part; it relates to the traditional code of *pulaaku*, requiring extreme reserve. Some mothers carry this reserve so far that at first other women nurse their babies. Beyoode does not leave her daughter for a second. She stays near her, seated on a mat, and welcomes women from neighboring encampments who come to see the new

Leaves of the good-luck *barkehi* tree

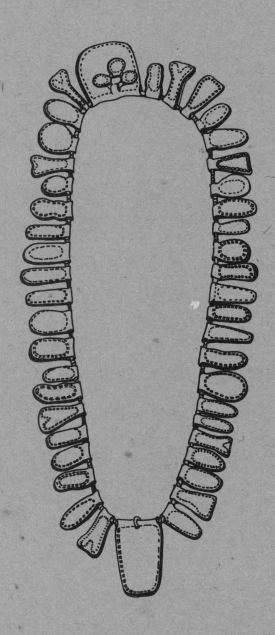

Necklace of talismans worn by nursing mother

mother. For them and for Kannde too, Beyoode prepares more *kunu*. The ingredients have been sent by the baby's father, Tambaya, who has been told of the birth but is forbidden to see his wife and child. For the rest, Kannde will be relieved of all domestic chores by her mother and the other women of the encampment. However, this will not stop her from climbing up on donkey back with her baby and riding with it placed before her, wrapped in a cloth, when the migration resumes, after one day.

Seven days after the child's birth, the *humto*, "the imposition of the name," takes place. This ceremony not only provides the child with a name; it legitimizes the child's paternity. It takes place in Kannde's parents' encampment. The father of the baby, Tambaya, may not attend. He is represented by members of his family, who bring the three calabashes of milk required for the ritual.

These calabashes are set down one meter from the calf rope. They are covered with flat woven lids, on which some good-luck *barkehi* bark has been placed. Beyoode, holding her grandson in her arms, squats between the calabashes and her *suudu*. Tambaya's brothers take their places and stand on the other side of the rope, facing Beyoode, holding pieces of *barkehi* bark in their hands.

The eldest brother repeatedly asks, "What is your name?" and then pronounces the name chosen for the child. The name is usually inspired by the conditions of birth. Since Kannde's child was born during a migration (*bangol*) he could be called Bango. But since he arrived during the rainy season, he could also have been named Diiye, which comes from the word *ndiiyam* (water). A child born on Monday (*Altine*) might bear that name. In this case, since the grandfather of the baby has many cows, the baby is named Riskwa, meaning wealth, to bring him luck.

This part of the ceremony lasts only a few minutes. Kannde is then given back her baby and squats down near the grandmother's *suudu*. Beyoode takes a calabash of milk in which *barkehi* bark has been immersed, sits facing her daughter, and with some milk, moistens the baby's head. Then she shaves the little skull with a razor, leaving only three round tufts of hair. As she works she drops the shaved hair into the milk. When the operation is finished, she takes the hair out of the milk and makes a small talisman for the infant to wear around its neck.

From this moment on, Kannde will herself be able to pick up and nurse her baby, but she will do so only in private, far from staring eyes. And as soon as the baby is nursed, she will place it on the ground and no longer tend to it. Even should imminent danger threaten the baby—a snake or scorpion, for example—she will not intervene if there is anyone else around. For four months she will be forbidden to carry the baby on her back. Her sisters or mother will do so in her place. At the end of the four months Beyoode, the grandmother, will seize Kannde and forcibly place the baby on her back, slipping a small branch of the *barkehi* tree between the two bodies. Kannde will feign tears, claiming that she wants to have nothing to do with this child.

During the following year, Kannde will not be permitted to address her son, Riskwa, and for his entire life will avoid calling him by name. All the rules governing Kannde's behavior are traditional and are enforced by the fear of shame (*semteende*) and the obligation of reserve (*pulaaku*). However, the rules apply only to a mother's first two children. From the third child on, a certain liberty is authorized in the relation between her and her children.

The migration continues day after day, under a blue sky swept by clouds that often mass and break in heavy showers. The ponds fill up, the pastures are greener than ever, the cows fatten and produce large quantities of milk. Thus, despite the wearying travel, everyone feels well. There is no shortage of worries, however. One day in mid-morning, as they approach Boka's encampment, Mokao and his brothers are startled by a chorus of moans. Mokao furrows his brow and, with a kick of his heels, spurs his camel on. The lamentations become clearer and fill the air.

As Mokao enters the encampment, he sees a body he instantly recognizes lying on a mat in the center of the clearing. It is Hasan, Boka's brother. Slowly circling around him are several dozen men and women, wailing mournfully. Mokao makes his camel kneel down and leaps to the ground. He draws near the group and takes hold of Boka as he circles the body, his face twisted with grief.

"Hasan!" Boka gasps. "He drowned in a shallow well in the middle of the pond."

He returns to his place in the circle, and is joined by Mokao and his brothers. The women clasp their hands behind their heads or raise them to the sky, repeating a rhythmic chant: "*En mboni yoo yoo* (Misfortune has befallen us)." Muna, Hasan's wife, falls to the ground screaming, and is overcome with hysteria. Others throw themselves into spiny bushes until they bleed. These dramatic manifestations of grief are called for by tradition.

Two elderly women approach the corpse and cover it with a mat. Reaching underneath the mat, they wash and dress the body, wrapping it carefully in a white shroud. Gao and Altine, as *ndotti'en*, select the location,

to the west of the encampment, where Hasan will be buried.

The men carry the body to the designated spot and bury it with the head pointing toward the south. The body is covered with a mat, branches, and then sand, and finally a few stones are piled in a pyramid above the grave. During the following four days, Altine, Boka, Huseyni, and all the dead man's family (the men and the women separately) receive visitors, who repeat as they draw near: "*En mboni yoo yoo* (Misfortune has befallen us)." They are offered only water to drink, and everyone remains silent.

The Wodaabe do not believe in an afterlife. They say that after death there is nothing. They therefore have no cult of ancestor worship. But they believe that a man who has many children, especially sons, survives in that his name and his features are perpetuated. They say that a man who dies leaving no children dies twice.

The continuance of the migration will not interfere with the rites surrounding Hasan's death being rigorously observed. One week after his burial the women of his family will prepare little balls of crushed millet mixed with sugar and distribute them to the mourners, and they will wash Hasan's clothes and give them away. Three months after the burial, Hasan's family will choose the most beautiful cow of his herd, the one he loved the best, and slaughter it. The meat will be offered both to members of his family and to neighboring encampments. Hasan's widow and children will not be allowed to attend this ritual or partake of the meat. But his three sons will inherit their father's herd, the eldest receiving the largest share. Until the children are old enough to take charge of their cattle, Hasan's brother, Boka, will care for them.

From the moment of Hasan's death, his widow, Muna, is obliged to remove all her jewelry and the clothes she customarily wears, and to undo her hair. For ten days she eats nothing and drinks only water. For five months she must remain at the encampment and keep her head lowered and covered by a cloth or an old garment of her husband's in order not to see the sun "from sunrise to sunset." On one foot she will wear one of her husband's sandals. A talisman against fear will be given her, as well as a knife and an ax with which to defend herself against the evil spirits of the bush. No man may approach her, and a terrible fate—the loss of his whole herd, or even death—may befall anyone who transgresses this interdiction.

Once the five months have passed, Muna will remove her husband's sandal and will again be able to dress her hair and wear her customary clothes. One year after

Hasan's death the *ndotti'en* will ask the widow if she wishes to marry one of her husband's brothers. If she refuses she is free to return to her family. In most cases widows accept this remarriage, which enables them to continue living with their children, since children must remain with their paternal family.

Hasan will not be forgotten by his family, and his name will be spoken often. It will always be spoken along with the formula "May Allah hail you."

Throughout the *nduungu*, August through September, the Wodaabe keep moving to the north. It is the heart of the rainy season. Soon the rains will become less frequent. That is when the celebrations that everyone is waiting for will take place. In the evenings visitors become increasingly numerous. A goat or a sheep is slaughtered in their honor, and the meat is shared among them. Conversations are animated. No one talks of anything except the *worso* and the *geerewol*—of dances and rejoicing.

Men and women busy themselves in preparation for the approaching ceremonies. Some have been to the market to buy everything they will shortly need. The men have procured tea, blocks of sugar, new leather saddlebags for their camels, handsome Tuareg saddles, brightly colored blankets, swords, spears to use in the ceremonial dances, tanned hides to make new *dedo*, colored wool yarn to decorate their conical hats, silver pendants, brass rings, and shells—chiefly cowries—for their hair. The women have found new wrappers and lengths of shiny colored material, shot through with gold and silver threads (with which they will cover their heads), calabashes that they will dye and decorate, and pieces of jewelry. Among those most highly valued are the heavy brass ankle bracelets worn by young girls. These are executed on commission by Hausa craftsmen and decorated by them according to the Wodaabe's specifications. There are also brass earrings, which the women embellish with yellow and red triangular-shaped pieces of glass.

As the ceremonies draw near, the women refurbish their possessions. They dismantle the beds and calabash tables, washing them with water and rubbing their various pieces with a red dye obtained by dissolving a vegetal powder, bought at the market, in water. Then they take the calabashes out of their woven cases and clean and repair them if necessary. Some are whitened with curdled milk and others dyed red and decorated with silver studs.

The men make necklaces and bracelets which they embellish with brass, colored glass beads, and shells. They also create numerous talismans which they hope

Brass anklets worn by a *surbaajo*, two on each leg

will set off their beauty or charm to good effect and attract women. They pay particular attention to the decoration of the ornaments they will wear during the dances. In the evening they continue their work while they chat, exchange jokes, tell tales, and play word games.

Everyone gathers around when Diiye and Jae start matching wits in one of these tests of verbal dexterity.

"*Taalee, taalee,*" says Diiye.

"*Taaleete!*" responds Jae.

Thereupon the two men launch into a rapid-fire series of questions and answers in which the last word of each question must be repeated at the beginning of the answer.

"Where is the goat?" asks Diiye.

"The goat is in the reeds," replies Jae.

"Which reeds?"

"The reeds in the river."

"Which river?"

"The river that is large."

"Large in what way?"

"Large in relation to the ponds."

"Which ponds?"

"The ponds of Modoro."

"Which Modoro?"

"The Modoro of the toads."

"Which toads?"

"The toads of Allah."

"Which Allah?"

"Allah of the sky."

"Which sky?"

Jae, beginning to tire, answers only by raising his hand above his head and saying, "That one."

Delighted by this unexpected twist, the gathering audience bursts into laughter. Drawn by the laughter, several children approach. Seeing them, Bango takes over and cries out, "*Taalee, taalee.*" To this, little Gado joyfully returns, "*Taaleete!*"

"I shall tell you," Bango says, "the story of the bull and the hyena.

"One day, a hyena has a baby. A short distance away, at the same moment, a cow has a baby. The hyena leaves to hunt and the cow to graze. Meanwhile, the little hyena meets the little calf, and, awaiting their mothers' return, they spend the day playing together. At nightfall the little hyena says to her friend, the calf—"

Here Bango speaks in a baby's voice:

"'You must go home, for if my mother finds you, she'll eat you up. She is very wicked.'"

In his normal voice he continues:

"The calf runs home. The hyena returns from the hunt and finds her little one. She asks her," Bango says in a booming voice, "'Whose hoofprints are these I see in the sand? Whom have you spent the day with?'

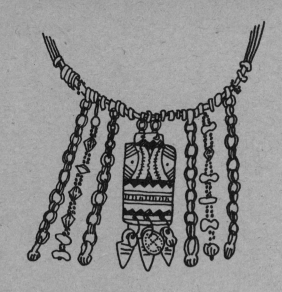

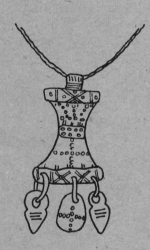

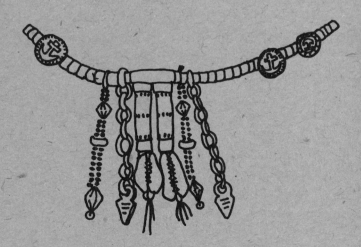

Dance necklaces made by Wodaabe of brass, leather, beads, and cowries

"The little hyena answers, 'I don't know. I don't understand. If you scold me, I won't nurse.' The hyena says, 'No, no, don't worry. It was only a joke,' and her little one comes to nurse. The next day, the hyena thinks about the hoofprints and sets out to follow them. But her little one, alarmed, says to her, 'No, no, don't do that! Or else I will not nurse this evening.' And the hyena leaves to go hunting, but on her way she discovers the mother cow's hoofprints and follows them."

"I bet that wicked animal is going to eat the cow," cries little Belti.

"Wait," Bango says. "The cow goes to graze, then rests in the shade of a tree. The hyena, continuing to follow the tracks, finds her at last beneath the tree. Meanwhile, the little hyena and the little calf are playing together again. At the end of the day, the little calf returns home and waits for his mother. The hyena comes home with plenty of meat, and says to her little one, 'I found a cow and killed it. Here is the meat.' Her little one replies, 'If that's so, I will not nurse.' The hyena says: 'I'm only joking, it's not a cow.' But the little hyena refuses to nurse."

"She's quite right," cries Gado indignantly.

"The next day," Bango continues, "the hyena again leaves to go hunting. The little calf comes to see his friend and discovers that the hyena has indeed killed his mother. The little hyena and the little calf agree to punish the hyena. They dig a large hole in the sand and cover it with branches and a mat. When the hyena returns that evening and calls her little one to come nurse, the latter says, 'Hin! Hin! If you don't come here, I won't nurse.' When the hyena approaches the mat she falls into the hole, and instantly the little hyena sets fire to the branches, burning her up."

The children let out horrified exclamations. Bango goes on, unperturbed: "The hyena yells, cries, whimpers with pain. Her little one claps her hands and calls her friend: 'Hey calf, hurry up, come see! My mother is cooking!' And in this way the little hyena and the little calf found themselves with no mothers. And they lived together, played together, ran together. Years went by, and they grew up. The hyena became stronger and stronger and her teeth began to hurt. She grew hungry for meat. One day the hyena returns from hunting and sees the bull, sated from grazing, resting. She comes from behind, stealing up close to the bull's rump—"

"Watch out! Watch out!" cry several children.

"But," Bango goes on, "just as she is about to bite, the hyena stops and says to the bull, 'My friend, we must part, for I'm likely to kill you. And if I don't kill you, you will kill me.' And the bull answers, 'All right, my friend. I agree, we shall part.' When the moment arrives to take leave of each other, the hyena says, 'My friend, the day you feel a light, warm breeze, that day I

shall no longer be alive.' And the bull replies, 'My friend, the day you feel a light, cool breeze, I shall no longer be alive.' And they part."

"And then? And then?" Gado asks, more and more intrigued.

"The hyena goes into the bush," Bango says, "and is felled by hunters, and the bull, immediately feeling a light, warm breeze, says to himself, 'Today my friend is no more.' He goes into the bush and arrives at a *worso*, where he is slaughtered. As the hunters are cutting up the hyena, they notice a quivering. The hyena has just felt a light, cool breeze and understood that her friend was no more."

Amee has not waited for the end of the story to slip away into the night, his herder's staff across his shoulders. He heads for the encampment of a bii Korony'en *surbaajo* named Modi, whom he had met at the market and whom he likes very much. He walks for two hours, laboriously because of his limp, before reaching her encampment.

Once nearby, he positions himself behind the encampment and begins to sing softly, pronouncing Modi's name. She does not appear, and Amee sings on tirelessly. Then, silently, he approaches Modi, who is lying on a mat near her mother's *suudu*. He touches her face, then withdraws and waits. Modi is wide awake but pretends to be asleep. And Amee, standing with his hands resting on his staff, observes her patiently. Finally he decides to go back to her again, crawling over the sand until he is right near her head. He murmurs softly, "I'm here, I'm waiting for you." Then he returns to his former post. Modi makes up her mind then to get up and go to meet him.

"Why didn't you come earlier?" Amee asks, "I have been singing so long for you."

"I didn't feel well," Modi answers.

Amee realizes that she is lying, that she says this because she does not like him. He asks her bitterly: "And now what are you going to do?"

"I'm tired, I want to sleep," the young girl answers.

Amee protests, "I've come a long way, a very long way. I walked a long way to see you. You can't just let me leave like that. You can't bring yourself to tell me you don't want me. I'm a man like the others. I'm no less than another. You're not tired. Simply tell me that you don't like me."

Modi remains silent. Then Amee declares, in a wounded tone of voice, "You would welcome even a barking dog if he came to see you. Then why not me? If you don't like me, I'll find someone else who will." He leaves, going out into the night to begin the long walk back to his encampment.

Meanwhile, under the direction of the *ardo*, the chief, the *ndotti'en* of the various encampments meet to discuss the date and location of the *worso*. Finally, one evening, the news breaks: the *ndotti'en* and the *ardo* have chosen the day and place of the *worso*. Everyone will leave tomorrow at dawn and in three days will arrive at the journey's end. Instantly, agitation and excitement reign in the encampment. Happiness seems within reach—the blessed period, the reward so longed for after months and months of hardship and superhuman effort. The nomads are at last to enjoy what they have suffered and borne so much for: the happiness of coming together again.

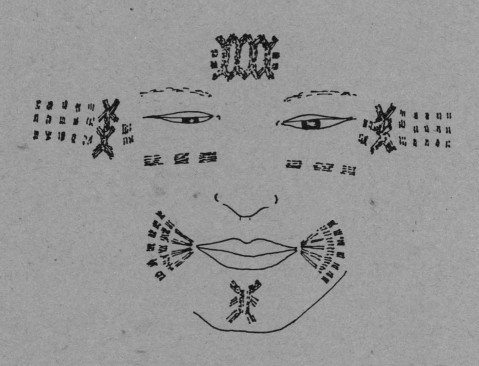

Female scarification patterns

During the long dry season when the Wodaabe depend on wells, their migrations are short. As the rains begin in the south and move to the north, the nomads "follow the clouds," traversing ancestral northward migration routes, finding new grass, ponds formed by the fresh rains, and the saline earth necessary for their animals' health. The cattle begin to thrive and milk becomes plentiful.

During the long migration, the Wodaabe may move every other day. Each time, they load all their possessions onto their donkeys, pack oxen, and camels. The women often carry on their heads calabashes of milk left over from the morning meal. Everything has to be unpacked again when the encampments are set up.

Every married woman has a pack ox to carry her ritual possessions—her *kaakol*, *elletel*, and ceremonial calabashes, often as many as fifty, nested in groups of ten. The rest of her possessions—bed poles wrapped in mats, sacks of millet, mortars and pestles, cooking pots, and clothing —are loaded onto other pack animals. Children and new mothers ride atop donkeys, often holding newly born animals on their laps. Though a nomad's belongings are relatively few, the beasts are laden to capacity when the group sets forth.

Men ready their camels, putting on saddles wrapped in bright-colored cloths
for protection. When there is no more
room on the donkeys and pack oxen, a
woman's possessions are sometimes
strapped onto the flanks of a camel.

As they migrate northward the Wodaabe move from pond to pond, watering their animals and filling their goatskins. Thinking ahead to the rainy season celebrations, young women begin to put on their bright brass anklets. But the men's camel saddles are still kept in their protective wrappings so that they will be in prime condition for the ceremonies.

To provide their animals with salt, some Wodaabe travel as far north as Teggidan Tessoum, the salt flats at the edge of the desert. There, hundreds of shallow holes are dug in the earth by local workers and filled daily with water. As the water evaporates, the salt crystallizes on the surface. It is collected by the local women, fashioned into cakes, and baked in the sun. This salt is also available in the markets that the Wodaabe frequent, brought there by camel caravans.

THE WORSO

The *worso* is a yearly occasion, lasting three or four days, when all the members of a sublineage gather together. Hundreds of men, women, and children, and thousands of animals—zebus, sheep and goats, camels, donkeys, dogs—arrive within a few hours at the chosen location, converging in an atmosphere of extraordinary disorder, confusion, even frenzy.

The women on their donkeys have been outdistanced by the more rapidly progressing herds. When at last they arrive, they dare not dismount lest the liberated donkeys get mixed up in the general pandemonium, but wait for some order to be established. Meanwhile they have a chance to chat about the various ceremonies that will take place during the *worso*. They begin with the *toko*, the ceremony of recognition of paternity, during which a bull belonging to the father is slaughtered and the meat is shared by the two families.

"I'm looking forward to little Riskwa's *toko*," says Tuwa eagerly, anticipating the excitement of the final ritual of the birth ceremony.

"I wonder what kind of bull Tambaya will offer his wife's family. He may have named his son Riskwa, but everyone knows his herd isn't worth much!" Fatiima scoffs.

"That's not true," Nebi protests. "Tambaya has fine animals, and he adores Kannde. He'd do anything for her and for her family.

"I remember the night when Kannde gave birth," she adds. "It was right in the middle of the migration!"

"For my part, I can't wait for the *koobgal* marriage of Mogoggo and Bello," Tuwa remarks. "And of Bello you can't say that he hasn't some handsome animals to present to his wife's family."

"Handsome animals!" mocks Fatiima, who has the

sharpest tongue of the three. "His herd is full of sterile cows and weak cattle. There's not a single one that could serve as a pack ox!"

"You'd do better to save that kind of criticism for tomorrow!" replies Tuwa. "As for myself, what I'm waiting for above all are the dances and dancers, and that's tonight."

"To think that I won't be able to attend!" says Nebi with a sigh, for she is still nursing her little Hadija, and may not leave her mother's encampment until the infant is weaned.

A short distance away, each holding a pack ox by its rope, Mowa, Beyoode, and Dulel also wait for the encampment to get organized.

"The men don't seem very handy today," Dulel remarks.

"What do you expect? The poor men, they're tired," Mowa answers.

"There's one who seems even more tired than the others," Beyoode says scornfully. "Look at Boka! He's falling asleep on his camel!"

"Boka has been constantly tired for some time now," murmurs Dulel, "to be exact, ever since he met Mariyama near Eggo Well."

"You shouldn't say such things," Mowa reproaches her.

"But everyone knows about it!" Beyoode exclaims. "For weeks now, I've heard, Mariyama has refused to open her knees to her husband. And she even slips her sandals upside down under her mat to rob him of his virility."

"All this is going to turn out badly," Mowa murmurs. Then, looking at the men, she adds, "I think we're going to be able to set up. It seems they've finally succeeded in making some order."

Indeed everything is gradually falling into place. The number of encampments is such that the line they form will be two kilometers long. As at each halting spot, the disposition of the encampments is in accordance with the masculine hierarchy. Thus all the encampments of

---

OPPOSITE: A Tuareg nomad arrives in full regalia to join the Wodaabe in celebration of the rains.

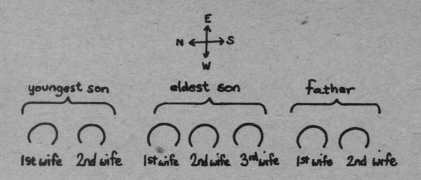

youngest son eldest son father

1st wife 2nd wife 1st wife 2nd wife 3rd wife 1st wife 2nd wife

the older families of the sublineage occupy the southern end of the line, and those of the younger families the northern end. Likewise, within each encampment the *cuudi* of the wives of the eldest of each family are located to the south, while those of the wives of younger brothers or of a younger son are located to the north.

Since the place each individual occupies during the *worso* is a function of his social status, the spatial organization of the *worso* makes instantly apparent the social situation of the various families and the status of the members of these families within a lineage.

Each of the two clans that make up the Wodaabe—the Degereeji and the Alijam—is divided into lineages, which are broken down into sublineages. Each sublineage is made up of families descended from the same ancestor, gradually augmented by men and women from other sublineages who have become associated with it by marriage or by choice. All the members of a sublineage consider themselves related, because for many generations they have occupied the same pastures and shared the same wells and migration routes. They are led by one chief, the *ardo*, who inherits the office but is subject to the approval of the men of his group.

A sublineage may include from one to three hundred members. If it grows too large, it can divide. Moreover, a family no longer wishing to follow its *ardo* is free to break off and join another group. Consequently, the social organization remains flexible and mobile. But the sublineages are endogamous: their members marry within the group, at least they do so in the arranged *koobgal* marriages. Relations between families belonging to the same sublineage are therefore very close. However, the encampments that make up a sublineage are separated from one another during the greater part of the year. The *worso* occasions the reconstitution for a few days' time of the social structure of a Wodaabe sublineage.

Shortly after arrival at the site chosen for the *worso*, the men lead their herds in the direction of the pastures and the pond. Meanwhile, the women, as usual, construct and arrange their *cuudi*. This time, however, there is an essential difference in the way the women proceed.

On this *worso* eve, Mowa unpacks her ceremonial calabashes, the treasure that she exhibits only on important occasions. She sets out on the table, one by one and with infinite care, the fifty calabashes that she has assiduously prepared during these last weeks: large ones, small ones, red ones, white ones, all decorated with consummate skill. In the center of the table she places her *kaakol* and *elletel*. At last, after months of waiting, she is able to exhibit her riches for the admiration of all. Presently, and throughout the *worso*, curious, envious, and sometimes critical, the women will pay visits to inspect and compare one another's treasures. This is the chance for the most uncharitable among them to criticize what they see. Old Kesso, Gao's sister, is the acknowledged master of this kind of criticism. However, for the most beautiful displays the women

Lineages of Wodaabe in Niger

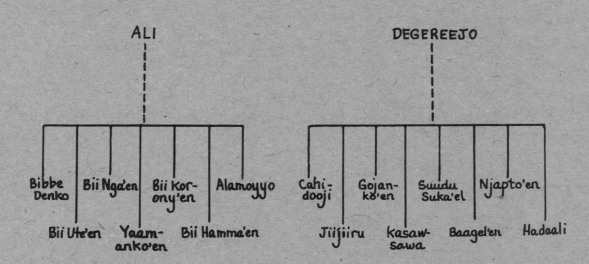

ALI

Bibbe Denko Bii Nga'en Bii Kor-ony'en Alamoyyo

Bii Ute'en Yaam-anko'en Bii Hamma'en

DEGEREEJO

Cahi-dooji Gojan-ko'en Suudu Suka'el Njapto'en

Jiijiiru Kasaw-sawa Baagel'en Hadaali

express their admiration by singing and performing a foot-stamping, hand-clapping dance.

The men begin to construct two ritual shelters to the west of the line of encampments, one *suura* for the *sukaabe*, one for the *ndotti'en*. These *suura* are long rows of branches set in the ground, before which the men spread a carpet of grasses. Here, twice daily, they will take their meals, brought to them by the women, walking in long processions, carrying on their heads calabashes of milk and millet porridge.

Toward late afternoon, everyone begins to prepare for the celebration. Men and women open the leather sacks in which for many months their most beautiful garments and jewelry have been stored. They take out wrappers and embroidered tunics, lengths of shiny material, bracelets and necklaces. Each person dresses according to age and sex; the younger men and women are freer than their elders to give rein to their imagination.

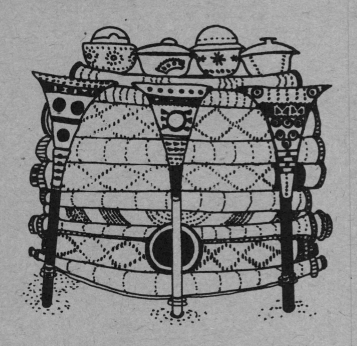

Portion of a married woman's possessions (mats and covered bowls) as displayed at a *worso*

After the evening meal, which takes place in their *suura*, the *sukaabe* light small fires, around which they sit in circles. They begin to make themselves up in anticipation of the *ruume*, the first evening dance of the *worso*. This important preparation is carried out meticulously and can take several hours. For the *ruume*, each dancer can make up differently. Imagination may run free, but always within the bounds of the Wodaabe's criteria of beauty, which call for lightening the skin, lengthening the face and nose, thinning the lips, and emphasizing the whiteness of the eyes and teeth. Toward these ends, a man covers the oval of his face with pale makeup, outlines his eyes with kohl, blackens his lips, and draws a line down the ridge of his nose.

When their makeup is complete, the young men wrap their heads in white turbans secured with dark-blue headbands containing talismans. To the headband they attach two long leather strips wrapped in brass and decorated with cowries, which hang down, one on either side of the face. But here too each suits his own fancy. Boka chooses to add a string of little bells that will jingle as he moves in the dance, and Agola adds a row of brass buttons from the French marine uniform.

The hour of the dance has arrived. Already some *sukaabe* are walking in small groups, holding hands, toward the spot where the *ruume* is to take place. Agola, Boka, and Bango, upon arriving at the dance ground, immediately join the circle that is forming.

The leader of the chorus already stands in the middle of the circle. He sings out a few words, after which the dancers, who for the moment remain immobile, repeat his words, varying the phrase. The chant is mostly

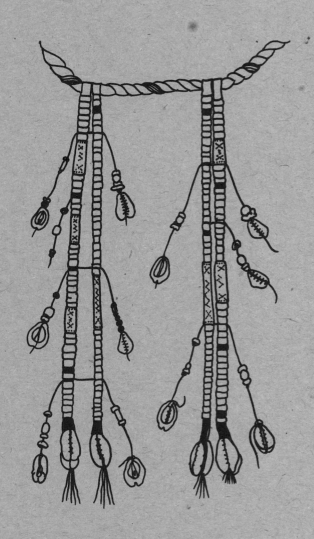

Decorative strips, made of brass-wrapped leather, beads, and cowries, worn suspended from male dancer's headband

147

pentatonic and could be transcribed approximately as follows: a *la* intoned by the leader, followed by the chorus's varied, mostly descending *sol mi re do* (or *si*) *la* response. The words of these songs are always verses in praise of a beautiful *surbaajo*. Tonight the song is about Juliyama: the leader sings the lines and the chorus repeats the last phrase.

"I sing of Juliyama, a girl lovely as water."
  "Lovely as water."
"A girl lovely as milk."
  "Lovely as milk."
"A girl with the eyes of a gazelle."
  "Eyes of a gazelle."
"She stands straight as a tree."
  "Straight as a tree."
"Her smile is enchanting, her teeth white as fresh milk."
  "White as fresh milk."
"Her face is as clear as the moon."
  "Clear as the moon."
"Her eyes shine like the sun."
  "Shine like the sun."

Drawn by the chant, the *surbaabe* move toward the circle in small clusters and surround the dancers. The leader continues to sing, occasionally placing his hands over his mouth to modify the tone. Suddenly the rhythm grows more pronounced. The dancers begin clapping their hands to a double beat, at times broken by sharp syncopation. Shoulder to shoulder, they begin to dance, moving slowly up and down with a slight, gliding sideways step so that gradually the entire circle

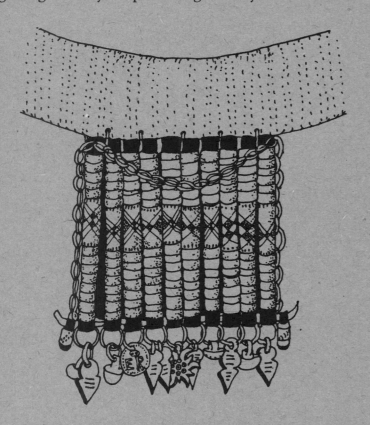

Brass-and-leather ornament worn by *ruume* dancers on the nape of the neck

rotates counterclockwise. Half of the circle intones a chant which the other half then repeats. One after another, small groups of dancers leap into the middle of the circle, all the while chanting and clapping hands to a much more rapid, syncopated beat. They punctuate their chant by stamping the ground with their feet.

The spectators, young and old, now crowd near. Mowa, Dulel, and Beyoode draw close to the circle, watching Bango, who rolls his eyes to show off as much of the whites as possible, and flashes his gleaming teeth in a smile directed to all the *surbaabe* who come within his field of vision.

Boka dances with equal fervor, and the string of little bells adorning his headband mark the beat of his every step. Already he has picked young Mariyama out from among the *surbaabe* surrounding the circle; he signals her discreetly by twitching the corner of his mouth in the direction he would like her to take. The young woman immediately leaves her companions and slips away into the darkness. A few instants later, Boka leaves the group of dancers and in turn wanders off. The disappearance of the couple seems to go unnoticed by the circle of dancers and spectators, and the dance continues.

Off to one side, the *ndotti'en* watch the spectacle of these tall figures swaying in the moonlight somewhat wistfully. They are too old to "enter the dance." Nearby, children play at being big people. They tie branches and grasses together and fasten them on their heads to represent the ostrich plumes waving gracefully on their elders' turbans. Then they paint their faces with ashes and, laughingly, throw themselves into an imitation of the adults' dance. When they get tired they snuggle up together on mats on the ground, rolled up in blankets, and pose riddles to one another.

"*Taalee, taalee*," says Gado.

"*Taaleete!*" replies Belti.

Immediately Gado asks his question at breakneck speed: "It is hung upside down but can't be turned over."

"A cow's udder," Belti returns, just as quickly.

"The cow walks from dawn to dusk but her tracks never cross."

"The horns."

"The big black beast who devours much millet."

Belti hesitates, searching for the answer. Baashi takes advantage of the moment to cut in. "The iron pot," he says.

Gado turns to him.

"A piece of wood with a tail, a head, and four branches," he asks.

Baashi scratches his head.

"The lizard," he proposes.

"No," Gado says, "it's the chameleon."

"Many cows and a single bull among them."

"I know," says Baashi proudly. "That's the stars and the moon."

"A great mouth, with children."

This time Belti is quickest. "The sky and the stars," he answers.

"A bush whose branches can't be used to make a fire."

All the children burst out laughing, and Belti exclaims, "An old man's beard."

At the dance ground the chant intensifies, punctuated by the clapping of hands and the sound of stamping feet. The sound acquires a strange hypnotic force; its swelling power echoes far off into the bush. From time to time tired dancers leave the circle and lie down on the sand to regain their strength so that they can reenter the dance.

The *surbaabe* gradually begin to rock back and forth to the dancers' rhythm, and to chime in with their high voices in certain passages of the chant. Finally, after three hours of the *ruume*, the *samri* announces that the dance is over, and slowly dancers and spectators disperse. But the evening is far from over. Groups form and stroll beneath the stars, while couples disappear discreetly into the darkness.

The first full day of the *worso* begins with the celebration of the year's births. While the first part of the ceremony for little Riskwa, the naming, had been conducted with all simplicity in his maternal grandparents' encampment seven days after his birth, this second and more important ritual, the *toko*, involves the slaughtering of a bull and brings together the many members of the two families.

However, tradition proscribes the presence of Tambaya, the father, at the *toko*. Nor may Kannde, the mother, attend; she leaves at sunrise, with her baby, for the bush, where she will spend the day. Later in the morning, Laabon, Kannde's father, and his brothers gather large tree trunks and pile them up behind the *suudu* of the grandmother, Beyoode, for a bonfire.

Tambaya's father, brothers, and uncles arrive at the encampment bringing their impressive herds of zebus for display. From among the animals the bull that is to be slaughtered is selected. This bull, called *tokoori*, must be big, beautiful, and healthy. The men first have to catch the animal, not a simple task, since the bull, sensing danger, runs for its life. This is an opportunity for the men to prove their agility and bravery. At last they succeed in catching it by grabbing its long horns. They then tie a rope around one of its legs and pull it to Beyoode's *suudu*.

They turn the bull over and tie its legs together. One of the men holds the bull's head sideways. Another digs a hole in the sand near its neck. Then, with a knife, a third man slits its throat. The blood spurts and flows in bursts into the hole. The bull shakes with violent contractions but dies quickly. A piece of its tongue is then cut out, to "keep it from talking," and this is hung on a tree branch. The legs are also cut off, at the knees. Then it is turned belly up and an incision is made from head to tail. The animal is skinned and the hide is laid on the sand. After this, it is carefully cut up and each piece is laid on a bush.

Each cut is meant for a particular person and has a precise symbolism. The front part of the bull is for the men, while the back part is for the women, since "the women follow the men." The young men, the *sukaabe*, receive the neck and breast, symbols of strength, while the *surbaabe* receive the heart, representing feeling and affection. Older women get the lungs and hooves as their share. The *ndotti'en* are given the liver, part of the stomach, and certain parts of organs in the fore part of the body, as well as the back of the neck. The belly is reserved for the mother and the scrotum for the father. Finally, a piece of the small intestine is given to Tambaya's brothers, who have cut up the animal. Once this work is done, the hide is entrusted to the *ndotti'en*, who will cut it into strips that they will distribute among the men. These strips will be used to make riding whips or sandals. In this fashion the division of the bull symbolically unites the two families.

The men roast their portions on wood skewers at the edge of the bonfire. By the end of the afternoon they will feast together in their *suura*. The women cook their portions in cast-iron pots and will eat them in their *cuudi*.

On this day the encampment will also be the scene of a ritual celebrating the marriage of Mogoggo and Bello. The rituals marking *koobgal* marriage are spread out over a long period, anywhere from fifteen to eighteen years. When Bello was five years old, his father went to see a cousin whose wife was pregnant and said to him: "If you have a daughter, I will take her as a wife for my son." Shortly after, a girl was born, and Bello's father returned to see the baby's father and reminded him of his request and its acceptance. Bello's father then gave young Mogoggo's father the sum of 500 CFA francs, and the young boy's aunts brought calabashes of milk, covered with leaves from the lucky *barkehi* tree, to the family of his "intended." This constituted, in fact, a "promise in marriage."

One year later, Bello's father offered a sheep to Mogoggo's parents. Six years later, during a *worso*, Bello's family made a gift of a bull to Mogoggo's family. It was slaughtered and the meat was shared by all. This sacrifice of a bull was repeated two years later at a *worso*. The bulls shared in this way are called *gai koobgal*, the bulls of the *koobgal* marriage. They serve to "tie together" the betrothed pair. From the moment of the first sacrifice, the children are named *kore* (spouse), and must adopt a reserved attitude: They may not speak to—and indeed must avoid—each other.

The third and last sacrifice marking the marriage of Bello and Mogoggo, which will take place during this *worso*, is the most important. It is preceded by the presentation of the animals offered by the boy's family to his future wife. Bello and Mogoggo, as well as their parents, are not permitted to attend this event. They hide separately in the bush so as not to participate in the discussions about the offered animals.

In the late morning, Bello's grandfather, brothers, and uncles arrive at Mogoggo's father's encampment. They are accompanied by their herds of zebus so that they can display their wealth to Mogoggo's family.

In the name of Bello's father, Bello's uncle moves into the middle of the herd and singles out, by striking them with a stick, those animals he intends for the young girl, which will be given to her on the day she sets up her own *suudu*. The women of Mogoggo's family—Mowa, Beyoode, Nebi, Fatiima, Tuwa, and others—then approach the designated animals and begin to make fun of them. Indifferent to their derisive remarks, Bello's uncle designates the animals to be given to Mogoggo: a pack ox, a heifer, and two cows.

"Did you see?" Fatiima taunts. "They offer only two cows, this family that is supposed to be rich!"

All these remarks are part of a set ritual, agreement on the number of animals to be given Mogoggo having been reached well beforehand between the families.

Bello's uncle takes the herds back to the family's encampment, leaving behind the bull that is going to be slaughtered.

The following morning the young women of Bello's family arrive at Mogoggo's family's encampment singing "*Hoowi-hoowi*" to consecrate the marriage. They walk in single file and carry calabashes of milk and a mat. All the women of the neighboring encampments come to join in the song. The mat is laid on the ground, and a little boy and girl—cousins of the married couple—are made to lie down and are then rolled up in the mat. A woman takes a swallow of milk and spits it on the

children, then hits them symbolically with a stick such as is used to beat milk. The children pretend to cry. All present then begin to voice their hopes for the absent young couple. They wish them, in particular, to have "a boy, a girl, a boy, a girl, a boy"—that is, many children.

For months following this ritual, both Bello and Mogoggo will remain with their families, and Mogoggo may have sexual relations with whomever she pleases, except her husband. With the onset of Mogoggo's first menstrual cycle, Bello's father will come to offer her father two heifers. As soon as this gift is made, Mogoggo will undo her hair and cover her head, and she will be forbidden to allow a man to come near her. If she goes into the bush, she will always be accompanied by a woman, and in addition she will carry an ax, to be used, if need be, to defend herself against evil spirits. This retreat will last three months.

At the end of this period, Mogoggo will be allowed once again to dress her hair. One night her husband will come in the company of a friend to find her. The friend will awaken the girl and begin to chat with her. Bello will intervene suddenly and try to take Mogoggo off with him. The girl will start to shout and cry, running for refuge to her parents. One week later Bello will return, alone this time, and take her forcibly into the bush, where the union will be consummated. Afterward, Mogoggo will return to her parents.

A few days later, an aunt and a brother of Bello's will come to get her and bring her to her husband. Again Mogoggo will shout and struggle. After one night spent at her in-laws, she will flee, returning to her parents' encampment, where she will stay for one week. After this, she will return on her own to Bello's encampment. But she will not yet have her own *suudu*. She will share her husband's mat near the *suudu* of her mother-in-law, on whom she will be entirely dependent.

Pregnancy, when it comes, will bring her back to her parents: at the end of the fifth month she will return, bringing with her three wrappers and a pair of sandals, and she will stay with them until her baby is weaned. Her husband will not be allowed to come to see her but will send her food from time to time. She will leave only when her mother decides that she may again live with him. Bello will then send her some wrappers, and his brothers will come to get her. She will return to Bello's encampment and will receive the trousseau given her by her mother, including an *elletel*, calabashes, wrappers, mats, a bed, a table, and household utensils. From her husband's mother she will receive a *kaakol*. Now she will build her own *suudu*. The two families will gather to celebrate the event—again with the young couple absent. Bello will braid a calf rope for his wife and entrust the milk cows to her care. Only at this moment will the status of married woman be conferred on Mogoggo.

Throughout the *worso*, the elders meet in their *suura*, where they spend hours holding counsel with the *ardo*, head of the sublineage, or resting. They are listened to because they have experienced much in life, and because they are the keepers of tradition. Their opinions are respected and their advice is generally followed. The Wodaabe say that "an old man sees everything, even if he is blind," while "a young man looks toward the distance and yet sees nothing."

When a member of the sublineage has been wronged, the *ndotti'en* call the victim and the guilty party to appear before them and talk for hours, seeking grounds for understanding. They do not inflict conventional penalties; they never go so far as to order corporal punishment. Their sanctions are most often limited to reprimands, but at times they decide on a fine payable in livestock.

Today a *suka* who was involved in a violent incident at the first evening's dance is brought by the *samri* before the council. The elders after reflecting and consulting decide to punish the troublemaker by confiscating his ceremonial finery. Instantly the young man prostrates himself on the ground and begins crawling toward the *ndotti'en*, asking their pardon, . . . and the punishment is immediately revoked. Another *suka*, who has greeted an elder without due respect, is called before the council and condemned to a fine of three calabashes of millet porridge.

At the end of the *worso*, the *sukaabe*, dressed in long robes that float in the wind, engage in exercises that display their skills. Mounted on their camels, they gallop at a furious speed behind the line of encampments, raising clouds of sand and dust. Their most highly applauded exploit is to make their camels advance, walking on the knees of their forelegs. Lastly they organize a race on camel back that will take them some twenty kilometers from the encampments.

On the final night of the *worso*, the *sukaabe* gather to dance the *ruume* for the last time, and when the dance is ended, they return, exhausted, to their encampments to sleep. In the middle of the night, a chant suddenly rises up, a deep chant that has not yet been heard: it is a traditional chant of the bii Korony'en. Led by their *ardo* and their *samri*, the bii Korony'en *sukaabe*, accompanied by their *surbaabe*, have arrived on camel back during the night, to the west of the Kasawsawa encampments. The reason for their visit is known to all: they have come to be invited by the Kasawsawa to the great *geerewol* celebration.

Hearing their visitors' chant, the Kasawsawa awaken. Immediately the *ardo* asks the women to gather mats and calabashes of water and milk and to follow the men heading to greet the new arrivals, repeating all the way: "*On jabbaama, on jabbaama!* (Welcome, welcome!)."

When the two groups are in each other's presence, they squat down facing one another and begin to exchange lengthy greetings. After this, the women place their calabashes and mats before the guests and the Kasawsawa return to their encampment.

The next morning the two groups meet, and the Kasawsawa, after having discussed the matter among themselves, propose to the bii Korony'en the date and place of the *geerewol*, the pageant of beauty.

Camel saddle (wood covered with red and green leather and cut-out silver) made by Tuareg smiths

With the coming of the rains, the nomads are in a mood to celebrate. Families gather. The men, clad in their most beautiful attire, arrive on camels in long processions, showing off the handsomeness and speed of their elaborately decorated mounts. In some of the celebrations, Wodaabe and Tuareg come together, the Tuareg women mounted on colorful leather-skirted donkeys.

Among the Wodaabe, reunited after almost a year of a relatively solitary existence, long, formal greetings are exchanged. Within the family groups there is much excited anticipation of the *worso*, the annual celebration of the numerous rituals that mark births and marriages. On such special occasions, animals are ritually slaughtered and the meat is shared by the families. Women unwrap and proudly display their ceremonial possessions, the most beautiful of which will be lauded in song and dance.

During the ceremonies, the elders play
an especially important role. Keepers of
tradition, they organize the rituals and
the dances, and make decisions on all
matters affecting the welfare of the lineage. A well-known *ardo*, Laamido Bayre
bii Tukay of the Degereeji clan, is shown
(*right*) arriving with his entourage to call
together a council of elders.

The slaughtering of a bull in honor of
the birth of a first son is an important
ritual of the *worso*. Large branches of
fallen trees are gathered for the fire on
which the meat, to be shared by the
families of the child's parents, will be
roasted.

For the married women the work of setting up the encampment includes preparing for display their most prized belongings—calabashes, *kaakol*, and *elletel* (*above*). Throughout the migration they have carried with them these treasures, well wrapped against the elements, toward the proud moment of their unveiling at the *worso*.

Clad in their finest attire, the women
and girls of a lineage stroll the encampments in groups, inspecting and apprais-
ing one another's possessions. At the
most beautiful displays they stop and
pay tribute in song and dance. Meanwhile the men race their camels, attracting large crowds, who wait eagerly at
the finish line.

THE GEEREWOL

The *geerewol* is a dance in which the handsomest young men of two lineages compete in beauty. This dance has given its name to a magnificent celebration that comes at the end of the rainy season. It is the climax of the year for the Wodaabe. An extraordinary atmosphere is created during the seven days of the *geerewol* by the fervor with which the Wodaabe throw themselves into the festivities. There are many *geerewol* going on during this time of year. For the period of the *geerewol* as many as a thousand people may be camping in the same location.

At this *geerewol* the Kasawsawa lineage are the hosts. They therefore arrive with their herds a day before their guests, the bii Korony'en lineage. They set up camp some distance from an immense pond—almost a lake—large enough to serve the needs of both the nomads and their animals. Each sublineage lines up its encampments parallel to the others; the lines may be several kilometers long.

Over all, the Kasawsawa will do everything possible to impress their guests, making an ostentatious show of their welcome. In reality there is great rivalry between the two groups. The Kasawsawa try to keep the bii Korony'en from being seen to advantage, especially during the dances, in order to protect their wives and daughters from being lured away. They have even been known to bury a wild melon (reputed to contain spells that will lessen the dancers' seductiveness) in the sand on the spot chosen for their guests' first dance.

On the first day of the *geerewol*, under the direction of the *samri*, the Kasawsawa *sukaabe* prepare the setting for the night dances. They construct a *suura*, which, as at the *worso*, is a simple screen (about ten meters long) consisting of a row of branches set into the ground. In

front of this they spread grass for the *ndotti'en* to sit on.

In the afternoon of the first day the bii Korony'en guests present themselves. Arriving from the west, as is traditional, they approach side by side in a row, mounted on magnificently outfitted camels.

Riding bareback on the camels, seated behind the *sukaabe* on their ornate saddles, are the *surbaabe*. All are protected from the sun by large umbrellas whose yellow, red, blue, green, and violet gores add kaleidoscopic color to the scene. The visitors have brought no herds with them, for their needs will be met by their hosts. They halt their camels some fifty meters from the *suura* and make them kneel down. Dismounting, they await the welcome of their hosts. The women draw back and stand patiently nearby.

The Kasawsawa *samri* and *ardo* advance to greet the new arrivals, saying, over and over until they reach their guests: "*On jabbaama, on jabbaama!* (Welcome, welcome!)."

The two groups of men squat down, facing each other, and engage in a long ritual of salutation. Then, leading their camels, the guests follow their hosts to the place assigned to them. Here the bii Korony'en men unload their baggage and unsaddle their camels. Then they head into the bush nearby to gather large branches of dead trees. These they set into the ground, and on them they hang everything they have brought along. After this, they unroll their mats and turn to making tea. During this time the women come to join them.

After sunset, Kasawsawa women, accompanied by an *ardo*, slowly approach the visitors in single file, carrying on their heads calabashes of milk and of millet porridge. They remove their sandals and, barefooted, lay the receptacles down in a line in the middle of the visitors' gathering place, where the guests, seated in circles in small groups according to age, will eat their meal. However, the bii Korony'en *sukaabe* may eat hardly anything; their calabashes must be returned half full. This is out of respect for the Wodaabe tradition of hospitality, which calls for a guest to eat little. As a

---

OPPOSITE: A young Wodaabe male dressed and made up for the *ruume* and *yaake* dances of the *geerewol* ceremony.

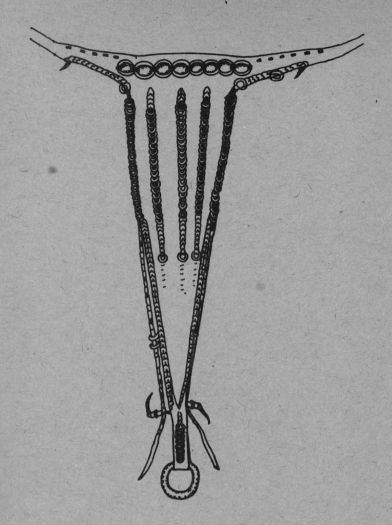

Back of a traditional leather *geerewol* belt decorated with brass rings

consequence, the *geerewol*, besides being a beauty contest, is also an endurance test.

Well after nightfall the bii Korony'en *sukaabe* begin by firelight to prepare themselves for the *geerewol* dance, which, by tradition, they, as guests, are to be the first to perform. Meanwhile some of the Kasawsawa *sukaabe* gather wood for the bonfire to light the dance and heap it up in a pile in front of the visitors' *suura*.

Making up is the most important preparatory act for the dance. But here—in contrast to the *ruume*—the makeup, red ocher mixed with fat, is the same for everyone, so that the dancers can be judged on the basis of beauty alone. Once his makeup is complete, each dancer puts on a woman's wrapper, pulling it snug around his hips and fastening it at the knees with a leather tie. This tie around his knees obliges him to take very short steps, which elongates his already long and narrow contour.

Around their necks the *sukaabe* slip colored bead necklaces, as well as a profusion of talismans, and over their bare torsos they crisscross long strands of white beads. They encircle their waists with several narrow belts, decorated with brass rings and cowries, and encircle their arms, above the elbow, with leather bands fringed with white hair from a male goat. After this they put on dark-blue headbands decorated with cowries and with a long fringe of white goat hair in back. Suspended from the headband, framing the face, are

pendent strips of leather ornamented with brass, brightly colored green and red wool, cowries, and white goat hair. Finally each dancer slips a long white ostrich plume into his headband.

Now many of the dancers down potions made from grasses and crushed barks mixed with milk. These are intended to increase their endurance, put them in a certain state of excitement, and, especially, as they say, "bring out their beauty." Not until they are entirely made up and dressed do the dancers arm themselves with the other essentials of the *geerewol* dance: a crescent-shaped iron ornament with little rings, which, attached to one ankle, resounds loudly as the wearer marks the rhythm of the dance, and a ceremonial staff topped with a metal wire shaped like an ax head.

When the dancers are ready, the Kasawsawa *sukaabe* light an immense fire in front of the *suura* and one of the elders advances to invite the bii Korony'en to begin the dance. Only the most beautiful of the *sukaabe*—about fifty—dare to participate. They approach the fire in little groups, taking the short steps necessitated by their bound knees. Under the direction of their *samri* they position themselves in a long line, shoulder to shoulder. Without moving at first, they begin to intone a chant unique to their lineage.

The chant begins on a low note sung by a soloist, a *do*, which is picked up by the other singers a fifth higher. Starting from this note, they make a series of phrases mostly on the notes *sol mi do*. The lows and highs overlap according to a regular rhythm, sometimes interrupted by sudden breaks or offbeats. According to the Wodaabe, these chants have the effect of "awakening" the potions they have taken, which "rise to the heart and show themselves in the blood."

The chant continues as the dance itself begins. On the beat, the fifty or so dancers, standing elbow to elbow in one line, rise to the tips of their toes, slightly bending their knees, and swing their arms forward in a long, elegant motion. At the same time they turn their heads alternately to the right and left, their broad, almost theatrical, smiles showing off the whiteness of their teeth, and they open their eyes very wide. As they dance, they tirelessly repeat the same refrain. Then they fall silent, and other bii Korony'en *sukaabe*, who are not dancing but stand in a row behind them, answer in chorus. There are several exchanges, which create an eerie, echoing effect.

Suddenly the chant ceases, and the dance changes beat dramatically. The dancers advance in short, rapid hops. The metallic sounds of the ornaments on their ankles strike out, depending on the movements of their feet, an

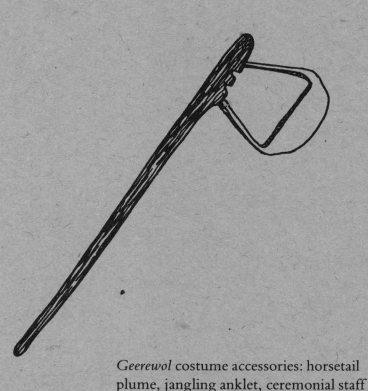

Geerewol costume accessories: horsetail plume, jangling anklet, ceremonial staff

alternation of strong and weaker beats. Low, dull thuds resound as they stamp the ground with the flats of their feet, at the same time brandishing and twirling their ceremonial staffs. Then, making a quarter turn to the south, still taking short, jumping steps, they form a long single file that advances several meters. With another quarter turn, to the same beat, the dancers return to their point of departure and realign themselves.

After about an hour of continual dancing, old Kesso, Gao's sister, dressed entirely in black, and wearing a turban given her by one of the elders, draws near the line of dancers, moving to the same rhythm. She pulls along a small wooden stool attached to the end of a chain. Arriving before the dancers, she stops and examines them one by one with critical and mocking eyes. Several women of the same age join her. In recognition of a dancer they find particularly beautiful, they bow almost low enough to touch his stomach with their heads, then, suddenly straightening up again, they shout, "*Yeee hoo!*" They make fun of the less well endowed dancers, criticizing their shortness or irregular features or unpleasing voices.

Old Kesso, letting loose, berates one dancer: "You're not fit to be in this dance! You're like a pack ox and I'm going to crown you with this stool and make you leave the dance."

During this mock contest—in which age has a chance to take revenge on youth and beauty—the dancers remain totally impassive. The spectators, however, comment on events with increasing animation.

"Have you noticed the third one in the row?" Fatiima whispers to her neighbor Tuwa, pointing. "He is as limber as a serpent. I think he's the one who will win."

"On the contrary, I think it will be the one next to him," Tuwa whispers back. "Look at that long, thin nose and high forehead! He's the most handsome of all!"

"But why don't the men bring more wood?" Hasana asks. "The fire is dying down. You can hardly see the dancers."

"They're letting it die down on purpose!" says Tuwa. "Or else they're using green wood so that the fire will burn badly. They're so afraid we'll find a dancer to our liking!"

Among the *ndotti'en* the criticism is far sharper. "Have you heard those voices?" Gao asks Altine. "They can't sing, these men!"

"There's nothing surprising about that," Altine returns. "It's well known that the bii Korony'en learned to sing from desert foxes."

The *sukaabe* are even harsher because they see potential rivals in the dancers from the bii Korony'en lineage. "Look at that one!" says Mokao disdainfully, pointing. "The dance is far from over and already he can barely stay on his feet!"

"And that other one, over there!" exclaims Bango. "With his short, crinkly hair, you'd say he was a son of a Hausa!"

"I think Dimoun will win," Laabon declares.

"It's always Dimoun," Bango grumbles. "And again he will steal our women."

"He hasn't won yet," Amee reminds them. "Let's wait to see what the *surbaabe* decide."

After several hours of uninterrupted dancing, the big moment has indeed arrived: the time has come at last to choose the winner or winners, who will be designated by *surbaabe* of the host lineage. A Kasawsawa *samri* points to three of the most beautiful *surbaabe* and signals them to leave the circle of spectators. At first the young girls act frightened and reticent, but with great authority the *samri* urges them to follow him as he goes off to one side.

Meanwhile the ten or so dancers designated as most handsome by Kesso and her friends leave the main group and exchange their ostrich plumes for horsetail plumes. They then regain their places in the dance, moving with light, graceful steps and continually changing their facial expressions to show off their beauty: they roll their eyes to display the whites and part their lips to exhibit their dazzling teeth.

The three chosen *surbaabe* now approach in single file. They slip off their sandals before penetrating the semicircle, advancing very slowly, their left hands held up beside their faces and their eyes demurely lowered. The *samri* places them in a line facing the dancers. They remain like this, standing motionless, for about five minutes, then slowly sink to their knees.

In the audience the excitement has reached such a level that most of the spectators can no longer restrain themselves. They stand up, and some even try to approach the *surbaabe*. Instantly the *samri* calls them to order, shouting and sometimes taking swings with his stick. Then he addresses the girls and gives them instructions. The crowd shrieks with delight. The dance continues toward its climax. A strange contrast is formed by the figures jumping to an ever more frenetic rhythm and the immobility of the *surbaabe* as they kneel, left hands held high, faces expressionless.

After about twenty minutes the *surbaabe* rise, and each one—gracefully swinging her right arm, and with her left hand still held against her left cheek—walks slowly toward the dancer she finds most beautiful and captivating. She almost touches him, then draws away, while the audience shouts out cries of enthusiasm. All three in turn choose handsome Dimoun, as Laabon had predicted: he is the winner of the contest. At once, over

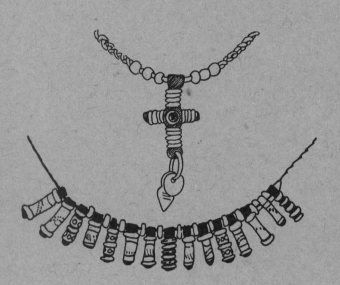

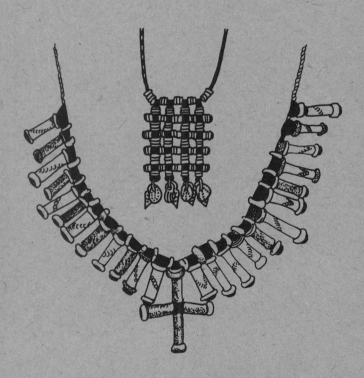

Necklaces of brass-wrapped leather worn during the dances

Libyan figures from the tomb of Seti I, c. 1330 B.C. (West Valley of the Kings, Egypt), bearing striking resemblances to plumed *yaake* dancers

the *samri*'s protests, the crowd mobs the dancers. This is the end of the dance, but the evening is far from over.

In the late afternoons and evenings of the following six days, the *sukaabe* of the two lineages will separately dance the *geerewol*. In accordance with custom, the guests will dance at least twice as often as their hosts. Another feature of the reunion of lineages is that every day, in late morning and again in midafternoon, some *sukaabe* of the two lineages take part together in a dance called the *yaake*, and each group of *sukaabe* are judged by the *surbaabe* of the other lineage. While the *geerewol* is the dance of beauty, the *yaake* is the dance of charm (*togu*). Clothing and makeup are not as precisely regulated as for the *geerewol*. Some dancers carry long ceremonial spears, and all wear turbans and embroidered tunics.

The dance itself is performed with the participants in a line, shoulder to shoulder, as in the *geerewol*. The spectators position themselves in a semicircle facing the dancers, men on one side, women on the other. *Samri* from both lineages direct the dance. In the *yaake* the dancers move slowly forward, alternately bending the knees and rising on tiptoe, while nodding the head in time with the beat. In this dance the emphasis is on facial expressions. They differ from one dancer to the next, but all have the same purpose: to bring out the whiteness of the eyes and of the teeth. And again the aim is to please the *surbaabe*, who observe the dancers from a distance. Clustered together, they stand in quiet, reserved postures.

The dancers wag their heads and roll their eyes or open them so wide that their eyes cross. They open their mouths and smile, then close and immediately reopen them, making their lips quiver. They also click their tongues and make kissing sounds. These noises are interspersed with the shrill, encouraging cries of the spectators. This joyful uproar strongly contrasts with the extremely studied rhythms of the *geerewol*.

When they have finished dancing or are tired, the *sukaabe* wander around in small groups, often holding hands. As they promenade, they meet young *surbaabe*, and many looks and a few words are exchanged. During the hottest hours of the day, men and women, young and old, retreat to the coolness of the big pond; they sit or lie on blankets under the trees bordering it, which are noisy with birds. Many dancers—the Kasawsawa on one side, the bii Korony'en on the other—sleep, exhausted both by their incessant dancing and by the lack of food.

Agola, Boka, and Diiye, still in their dance array, prepare very strong tea with the last of their provisions. All three are at the end of their strength, but they would not show it for anything in the world. Besides, their bii Korony'en rivals—who have danced twice as much—seem even more tired.

"Did you see their last *ruume*?" Agola asks. "There were two who left the circle in the middle of the dance. And it was not to go and meet some *surbaabe*! It was to go and sleep."

"Even Dimoun looks tired," Agola says. "I wonder if he'll be the best right to the end. In my opinion, no bii Korony'en will be able to hold on very long."

While some rest at the pond's banks, in the Kasawsawa encampments work continues: the herds must be tended, taken to pasture, and watered. In addition, meals must be prepared and the cows milked. But all seize every free moment to break away from their chores, especially

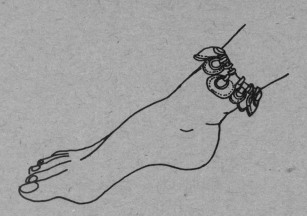

Ankle bracelet with talismans
worn to increase charm

in the evening, for the *geerewol* dances. These dances attract more people every day and give men and women from different lineages a chance to meet. Here couples make the fleeting encounters far from the eyes of their families that may lead to a brief sexual interlude or even to a *teegal* marriage. An unhappy wife who wishes to leave her husband may find a lover who will take her to his encampment and marry her.

With just such hopes, Koki, a young bii Korony'en whom Agola had met at the Intawella market, went with a few girl friends to the *geerewol* dance in which Agola was spiritedly taking part. Agola's and Koki's eyes met several times, and each time she lowered her head.

The following day, Agola and Koki saw one another again, on the banks of the pond. With his eyes Agola indicated an isolated spot where they might meet. There they talked together a long time. Koki is married to Banyi, who has treated her badly ever since taking a second wife, whom he preferred. Agola already had two wives. One, he said, was lazy, kept her *suudu* badly, and did not take proper care of her children; the heart of the other was not good, was "black like a moonless night." He no longer loved them. That evening, Agola again danced the *geerewol* with other Kasawsawa. Koki was there, among the women of her lineage, observing him.

As soon as the dance ended, Koki left her friends and went into the bush. Agola, fresh from the dance, wasted no time in joining her at their appointed spot, carrying a mat and a blanket lent him by Boka. On a level area of sand, far from any trees that might hide a snake or a scorpion, the lovers spread out the mat and lay down, side by side, pulling the blanket over them. They began to talk. Suddenly they heard footsteps drawing near.

They fell silent and lay absolutely still. The sound of the footsteps stopped not more than a couple of meters away. They held their breath. Finally the last steps moved off. If they had been caught, Koki would have been beaten by her husband. The danger past, they hastily made love, Koki covering her eyes with her forearm in a reflex gesture of *pulaaku* (reserve). Wodaabe men do not like women who give themselves too quickly, too easily, or with too much ardor. They say such women lack *munyal* (patience) and *semteende* (shame).

The next day Koki and Agola saw one another from a distance, but avoided contact all day in order not to arouse suspicion. That evening it was the bii Korony'en's turn to dance the *geerewol*. As Koki could not attend a dance by *sukaabe* of her own lineage, she stayed in her *suudu*. Her husband, however, was dancing. Agola took advantage of Banyi's absence to take Koki quickly and stealthily to his encampment. There, he had made everything ready to celebrate a rapid and secret *teegal* marriage. A ram was slaughtered and shared by members of Agola's family.

Upon his return from the dance Banyi realized at once that his wife was gone. He immediately alerted his brothers and cousins, who set off in pursuit of the missing wife. Asking around, they soon learned that Agola and Koki appeared to be on intimate terms. Banyi's brothers ran to Agola's encampment. But Agola had disappeared into the bush with his new wife, in order to avoid a confrontation with Banyi and his family. After hours of searching, Banyi conceded the loss and returned home.

Luckily for her, Koki has no children. Otherwise she would have had to leave all but the very youngest with their father. But in her haste she did have to leave behind her ritual possessions, since they were too difficult to transport.

"Don't worry," Agola said, "I'll buy you new calabashes at market. And later I'll give you some cows of your own."

The end of the *geerewol* is near, but this seems only to increase the gaiety and excitement. Everywhere there is dancing, shaking, stamping, singing. The most artful makeups melt into the streams of sweat that roll down faces. The lightheartedness is total. But the first signs presaging the end of the celebration appear. Under the cloudless lavender-blue sky the harmattan once again begins to blow long, hot gusts of wind out of the desert.

The moment has arrived to begin the last dance. It goes on all night. Only those dance it from start to finish who have succeeded in withstanding both fatigue and hunger. Some collapse in the middle of the dance.

At dawn the *surbaabe* return once again to designate the victor.

A few hours later, just before departure, the Kasawsawa *ardo*, who has slaughtered several bulls to honor the guests one last time, has the meat roasted on tree branches over a fire. When the meat is cooked, the pieces are brought by the Kasawsawa to their guests, along with calabashes of milk. Again, the guests hardly touch what is offered them, each one taking but a small piece of meat and a sip of milk.

This farewell meal takes place in late morning. Immediately afterward, the bii Kirony'en take their belongings down from the tree branches where they have been hung, organize their baggage, and load their camels. Then, in the middle of the *suura*, the bii Korony'en *samri* sets into the ground a branch from the good-luck *barkehi* tree. On it the *surbaabe* of his lineage have hung many small pieces of jewelry: colored bead necklaces, rings, shells, and bracelets. This brightly decorated branch, a gesture of thanks and respect to the Kasawsawa, their hosts, is intended for the children.

The moment has arrived for parting formalities. The men squat down in two facing groups. The bii Korony'en guests thank their hosts at great length and wish them good luck and happiness, while the bii Korony'en *surbaabe* are already moving off into the bush, walking with short steps in single file.

Then the men separate. The bii Korony'en take their camels by the reins and leave slowly on foot, heading toward the west. The Kasawsawa return to their encampments, regroup animals and pack their belongings, devoting special care to their *geerewol* finery, which will not be used for a whole year.

The rainy season is over, and so are the celebrations that came with it. Soon the grass will yellow, the ponds will shrink, and the Wodaabe will return to the vicinity of the wells, which they will reach at the end of a month of migration. The cows will grow thinner, milk less abundant, life harder. But during the nine months of ordeals that lie between this moment and the new rains, the Wodaabe will hold in their hearts the memories of the days full of wonder that they have just experienced.

And there is something more deeply rooted and more sustaining that will fortify them: the freedom to follow the way of their tradition.

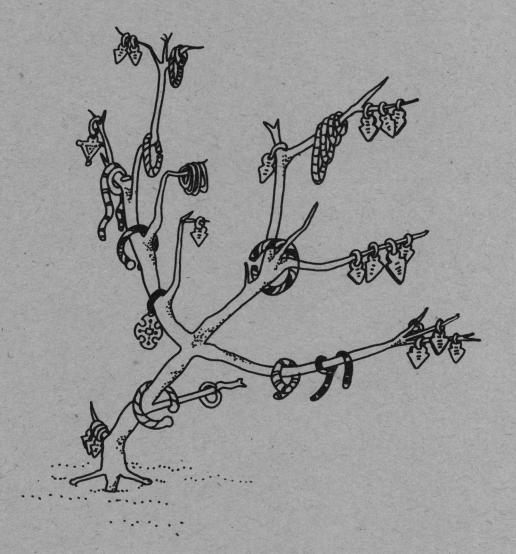

Symbolic branch of the *barkehi* tree set by the departing guest lineage into the ashes of the fire that lighted the *geerewol* dances

Geerewol is the name both of a dance and of the seven-day celebration uniting two lineages of the Wodaabe and held near the close of the rainy season. In the *geerewol* dance the most handsome males of one lineage compete against one another, presenting themselves to the women of the other lineage, who admire, criticize, and judge them. The winners are selected by the three most beautiful young women. Performed every afternoon and night for seven days, the dance is a kind of endurance test. Several other dances are performed during the *geerewol*: the *ruume*, a circle dance with rhythmic chanting and clapping, and the *yaake*, in which the dancers compete in charm, personality, and magnetism rather than in beauty alone.

The *geerewol* celebration begins with the arrival of the guest lineage, who settle under trees in an area designated by the *ardo* of the host lineage. Possessions are hung on the branches of trees. Over the next seven days young men and women find time to relax together, drink tea, and prepare their costumes and makeup for the dances.

Conforming to the Wodaabe criteria of beauty, male dancers lighten their skins with a pale yellow color, blacken their lips and eyes with kohl to bring out the whiteness of their teeth and the whites of their eyes, run a long line from forehead to chin to lengthen the nose, shave their hairlines to heighten the forehead, and decorate the cheeks with small patterns of dots and circles.

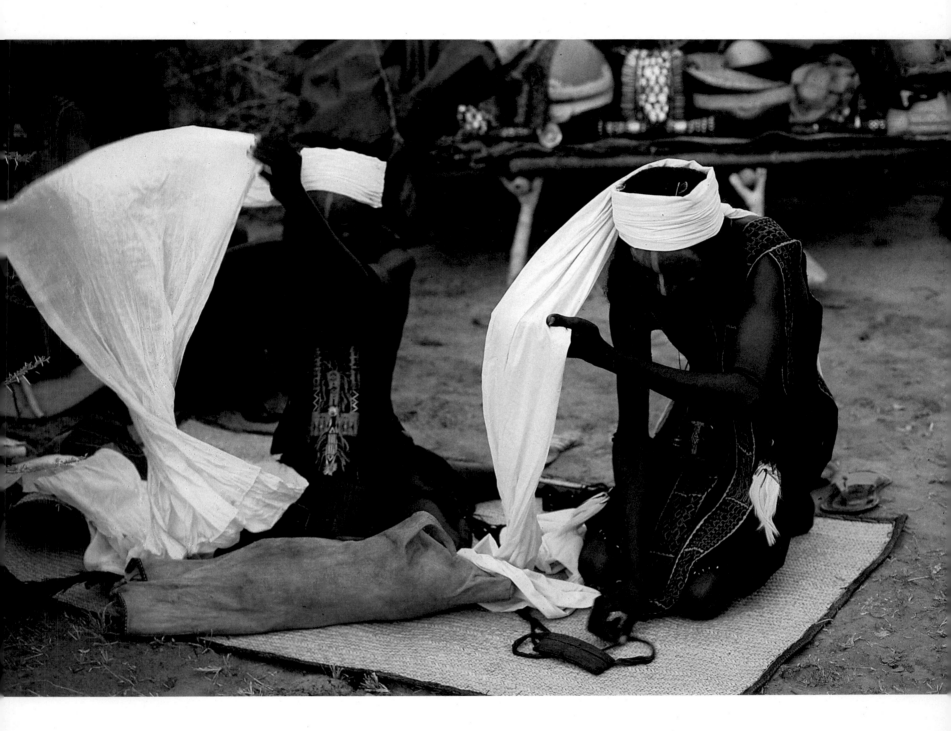

From wrapping the turban to final inspection in a hand-held mirror, dancers give painstaking care to every detail. Their women have spent months embroidering the tunics they wear. Beautifully crafted knives, spears, swords, leather purses, and silver ornaments have been purchased from Tuareg smiths. Leather talismans are worn to ensure beauty, guard against jealousy, heighten appeal. Shiny objects such as zippers and locks, watchbands, and empty cartridges are incorporated into costumes.

Young women take equal care; they polish their multiple earrings and bracelets, arrange their head wraps, and flourish colorful umbrellas.

Freshly made up, the young men and women gather for the *ruume*, the first circle dance of the *geerewol* celebration.

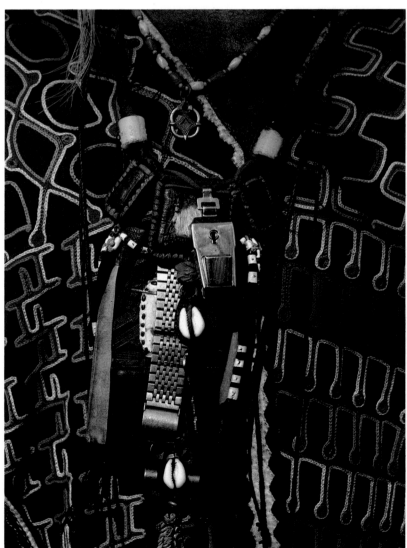

In the *yaake* the dancers try, primarily through facial expression, to surpass one another in charm, personality, and magnetism. Standing side by side facing their audience, they widen their eyes, roll their eyes to expose the whites, show off their teeth in broad, exaggerated smiles, make clicking sounds, puff and vibrate their cheeks, and pucker their lips. Every few seconds their expressions grow more extreme and frenetic. To emphasize their height, the dancers slowly advance on tiptoe toward the spectators. A dancer knows that he has been judged outstanding when an old woman dashes toward him, yelling "Yeeee hoo!" and gently butts him in the torso.

Between dances there is time for resting under the trees, drinking tea, and preparing for the *geerewol*, the climactic dance in which the young men compete in physical beauty. Side by side, they present themselves: they all wear ocher makeup on their faces; tight wrappers around their hips, bound at the knees; strings of white beads crisscrossing their bare chests; and white ostrich plumes topping their headdresses. In the dance, quiet passages alternate with frenzied jumping and stamping.

The three most beautiful young women of the guest lineage act as judges. Brought before the line of dancers they kneel modestly, left hands held up as if to conceal their scrutiny. A number of the dancers withdraw; those remaining are given white horsetail plumes to replace their ostrich feathers. After a period of observation the young women rise, and each one, with a slow swinging movement of the right arm, advances toward the dancer of her choice. The dancers try in every possible way, with bodily movement and facial expression, to attract the young women. The crowd goes wild with excitement.

The seventh evening marks the end of the *geerewol*, and the young men dance until sunrise. The morning after the last dance, the guest lineage departs. The rainy season celebrations leave the Wodaabe rich memories to fortify them through the long dry season ahead.

ACKNOWLEDGMENTS

Recording the Wodaabe way of life would not have been possible without the generous cooperation and assistance of Le Président du Conseil Militaire Suprême du Niger, Chef de l'Etat, Colonel Senyi Kountché, and of the following authorities in Niger: L'Institut de Recherches en Sciences Humaines; Diouldé Laya of the Centre d'Etudes Linguistiques et Historiques par Tradition Orale; Mahaman Abdu Maikano of the Centre d'Alphabétisation; the Embassy of the United States of America and USAID; the Embassy of Belgium; the Embassy of Canada; the Catholic Mission in Bermo; and Fougerolles and SATOM (Société Anonyme Travaux Outre-Mer).

We thank all our Wodaabe friends, especially Mokao bii Gao and his family, for welcoming us into their lives, and we should like to single out for mention, because of the special efforts they made in our behalf, the following lineages: Kasawsawa, Gojanko'en, bii Nga'en, bii Korony'en, Jiijiiru, Njapto'en, Yaamanko'en, and bii Hamma'en.

For assistance and hospitality during our expeditions into the field we are grateful to Richard Graille, Wendy Wilson, Angela Fisher, Annie Colas, Brigitte Butel, Pilot Dominique Pollus, Patrick Paris, Anne-Marie Wright, François Pradines, Danielle Donat, Jean-Pierre and Mary Kaba, and Roland Desbois. For technical aid we are indebted to E. Leitz, Inc., and Nikon, Inc.

At Abrams we should like to express our appreciation to Ruth Eisenstein for her perceptive editing, to Patrick Cunningham for his sensitive design, and to Robert Morton for his guidance and creative involvement from the inception of this book.

Above all, we owe the realization of our book to the devotion and commitment of Marie-Paule Tran-Verpoorten, Odette and Jacques van Offelen, Frédéric de Limelette (the author's husband), Stéphane Jourat, Mark Hukill, Tran Hong Cam, Toby Eady, Anne de Margerie, Leo Beckwith, and the late Betty Beckwith, whose loving encouragement never wavered, even during the illness that took her life.

M.v.O.
C.B.

Note. The following books provided useful background material: Brandt, H., *Nomades du soleil*, Lausanne (Clairefontaine), 1956; Dupire, M., *Peuls nomades (Etudes descriptive des Wodaabe du Sahel Nigérien)*, Paris (Institut d'Ethnologie), 1962; Laya, D., *La Tradition peule des animaux d'attache*, Niamey (IRSH) 1974; Maaliki, A., *Beldum: Bonheur et souffrance chez les Wodaabe*, Niamey (Mission Catholique); Stenning, D.J., *Savannah Nomads: A Study of the Wodaabe Pastoral Fulani of Western Bornu Province, Northern Region, Nigeria*, London (Oxford University Press), 1959.

M.v.O.